## Praise for *The Hurt Locker*

"It's extraordinary filmmaking."
—Manohla Dargis, *The New York Times*

"*The Hurt Locker*'s verisimilitude begins with the lean and com-
pelling script by Mark Boal. The story asks difficult questions
about heroism's costs and demands, about what war does to soldiers, and about damage that may be impossible to rectify or
repair. By the time this remarkable film comes to an end, we feel
it in our souls."                        —Kenneth Turan, *Los Angeles Times*

"Mark Boal has written a strong, awards-caliber script that nails
every telling detail and unfolds with dazzling virtuosity. It is cause
for celebration."                        —Peter Travers, *Rolling Stone*

"It deserves to stand as one of the defining films of the decade.
Bigelow and screenwriter Mark Boal pull us along with them,
insistent that we see war as soldiers do, in all it's brutal, romantic,
senseless, predictable, terrifying and even addictive ways."
—Elizabeth Weitzman, *New York Daily News*

"Watching it, you feel you're in the presence of art completely of
the moment and also aesthetically new. *The Hurt Locker* redefines
war-film electricity."                        —Michael Sragow, *Baltimore Sun*

"[*The Hurt Locker*] enters the pantheon of great American war
films."                        —Mick LaSalle, *San Francisco Chronicle*

# THE HURT LOCKER

## Screenplay by
## Mark Boal

## Introduction by
## Kathryn Bigelow

A Newmarket Shooting Script® Series Book
NEWMARKET PRESS • NEW YORK

FIRST EDITION

10  9  8  7  6  5  4  3  2  1

ISBN: 978-1-55704-909-4

Library of Congress Catalog-in-Publication Data available upon request.

QUANTITY PURCHASES

Companies, professional groups, clubs, and other organizations may qualify for special terms when ordering quantities
of this title. For information e-mail sales@newmarketpress.com or write to Special Sales, Newmarket Press, 18 East
48th Street, New York, NY 10017; call (212) 832-3575 ext. 19 or 1-800-669-3903; FAX (212) 832-3629.

Website: www.newmarketpress.com

Manufactured in the United States of America.

OTHER BOOKS IN THE NEWMARKET SHOOTING SCRIPT® SERIES INCLUDE:

About a Boy: The Shooting Script
Adaptation: The Shooting Script
The Age of Innocence: The Shooting Script
American Beauty: The Shooting Script
A Beautiful Mind: The Shooting Script
The Birdcage: The Shooting Script
Black Hawk Down: The Shooting Script
The Burning Plain: The Shooting Script
Capote: The Shooting Script
The Constant Gardener: The Shooting Script
Dan in Real Life: The Shooting Script
Dead Man Walking: The Shooting Script
Eternal Sunshine of the Spotless Mind:
    The Shooting Script
Funny People: The Shooting Script
Gods and Monsters: The Shooting Script
Gosford Park: The Shooting Script
Human Nature: The Shooting Script
Juno: The Shooting Script

Knocked Up: The Shooting Script
The Ice Storm: The Shooting Script
Little Miss Sunshine: The Shooting Script
Margot at the Wedding: The Shooting Script
Michael Clayton: The Shooting Script
Milk: The Shooting Script
The People vs. Larry Flynt: The Shooting Script
Punch-Drunk Love: The Shooting Script
The Savages: The Shooting Script
The Shawshank Redemption: The Shooting Script
Sideways: The Shooting Script
Slumdog Millionaire: The Shooting Script
The Squid and the Whale: The Shooting Script
Stranger Than Fiction: The Shooting Script
Synecdoche, New York: The Shooting Script
Taking Woodstock: The Shooting Script
Traffic: The Shooting Script
The Truman Show: The Shooting Script
War of the Worlds: The Shooting Script

OTHER NEWMARKET PICTORIAL MOVIEBOOKS AND NEWMARKET INSIDER FILM BOOKS INCLUDE:

Angels & Demons: The Illustrated Movie Companion
The Art of Monsters vs. Aliens
The Art of X2*
The Art of X-Men: The Last Stand
Bram Stoker's Dracula: The Film and the Legend*
Chicago: The Movie and Lyrics*
Dances with Wolves: The Illustrated Story of the Epic Film*
Dreamgirls
E.T. The Extra-Terrestrial: From Concept to Classic*
Gladiator: The Making of the Ridley Scott Epic Film

Good Night, and Good Luck: The Screenplay and History Behind
    the Landmark Movie*
Hotel Rwanda: Bringing the True Story of an African Hero to Film*
The Jaws Log
The Mummy: Tomb of the Dragon Emperor
Ray: A Tribute to the Movie, the Music, and the Man*
Saving Private Ryan: The Men, The Mission, The Movie
Schindler's List: Images of the Steven Spielberg Film
Superbad: The Illustrated Moviebook*
Tim Burton's Corpse Bride: An Invitation to the Wedding

*Includes Screenplay

# CONTENTS

Introduction by Kathryn Bigelow                    vii

The Shooting Script                                  1

Stills                              following page 86

Production Notes                                   115

Cast and Crew Credits                              126

About the Filmmakers                               133

# INTRODUCTION

## KATHRYN BIGELOW

In the winter of 2004, when Baghdad was one of the most dangerous places on the planet—a site of daily explosions, gunfights, and kidnappings—the city was, for the few Western journalists working there, an absolutely lethal place to work. So it was with considerable trepidation that I wished luck to my friend, reporter and screenwriter Mark Boal, when he told me that he had decided to go to Iraq to cover the war firsthand.

As a passionate investigative reporter, Mark had his eye on a little-known unit in the Army, the Explosive Ordnance Disposal team (EOD), aka the bomb squad, which was then playing a pivotal part in the military's attempt to contain the growing threat of roadside bombs, the so-called Improvised Explosive Devices (IEDs). Such was the nature of his choice to cover this high-risk unit that minutes after landing in Iraq, he was asked by Army officials to sign a "Hold Harmless" contract and provide his blood type and religious preference for a funeral.

For weeks he rode with EOD soldiers into hotly contested areas of the city, seeing in their daily battles with roadside bombs a side of the war that had not been documented before. By day, he witnessed and survived ambushes and IED attacks, not to mention random acts of cultural dislocation with the residents of Baghdad. At night, the base he slept in was bombarded with rockets and mortar rounds. Through it all, he gained an insider's perspective on what these bomb squad soldiers were living through, in a foreign country, halfway around the world.

Shortly after he returned from Iraq, Mark was determined to bring the story of what he'd seen to a wider audience. He proposed writing a fictional movie about the bomb squad, set in the real world. The idea, he said, would be to capture Baghdad's lethality while also telling the story of the young men tasked with what was probably the most dangerous job in the world. I thought it was a fascinating idea. We developed a shared vision for the film: an intense, naturalistic, soldier's-eye view of the conflict. In order to protect this approach and limit committee reaction to the tough material, we also decided to pursue the project independently, without any studio support. For Mark, that meant he'd be writing without any initial payment. He readily agreed and set out to write "a spec."

After reading the finished *The Hurt Locker*, I felt the excited rush of encountering an unforgettable script. It was both a probing character study, with the invention of Sergeant James and character arcs that radically unfolded in the reader's heart and mind, and, at the same time, it was a nerve-shredding combat thriller, with an innovative structure built out of authentic detail. It not only put one on the ground in Baghdad, to feel its relentless threats, but it also, quite subtly and brilliantly, became a meditation on existential themes of life and death, courage and manhood, war and human nature. In short, it was original and electrifying—and I knew it would be my next movie.

For his part, Mark felt so passionately about the project that I asked him to join me as a producer of the film. He jumped at the opportunity, and proved to be a natural producer, guiding the production through many logistical and technical challenges with the same commitment to excellence that he showed by going to Baghdad. The benefits were also aesthetic: with both of us as producers we were able to maintain an unusual level of control over *The Hurt Locker*'s creative destiny, from inception to the editing room.

Eventually, we raised a modest amount of independent financing, located the production in the Middle East, and cast a trio of talented young actors and several industry veterans, who signed on based on the strength of the script. By June 2007, we found ourselves in and around the city of Amman, Jordan, and Mark's writing came to life before our eyes. Although we were miles from home, shooting in punishing temperatures with the grit of sand in our eyes and teeth, the screenplay was the steady hand that led the way.

—September 2009

# The Hurt Locker

By

Mark Boal

June 7, 2007

Shooting Draft

**BLACK SCREEN**

Arabic man YELLING over a bull-horn.

**TITLE:**

**The rush of battle is often a potent and lethal addiction, for war is a drug. - Chris Hedges**

The loud BUZZ of an electric engine and the CRUNCHING of wheels traversing rough terrain. Then SIRENS, HORNS, SHOUTS.

As the din intensifies, the quote recedes.


**FADE IN:**


**EXT BAGHDAD STREET DAWN - ROBOT CAM POV**

*A grainy, low-resolution view of a dusty dirt road. We're low, just inches off the sun-washed ground, and moving fast.*

ZOOMING down a street littered with the refuse of war: spent munitions, rubber bits, animal waste -- all of which, from this odd, jarring perspective, looks gigantic, monstrous.

We approach a crumpled COKE CAN, the white 'C' growing enormous on the screen, filling the screen like a skyscraper, SMASH into the can and barrel ahead.

A RAG flutters, blocks our view, then flies away as we pop over a bump, catching air and a flash of the horizon line, BRIGHT SUN, then landing hard and continue zipping down the dusty road.

                                                    CUT TO:


**EXT BAGHDAD STREET - DAWN**

A rushed, disorderly evacuation. Iraqi POLICE and SOLDIERS herd civilians away from some unseen danger.


**INTERCUT:**

A remote controlled TALON ROBOT (about a quarter million dollars of military-grade bomb squad electronics, aka 'the bot') whose SMALL VIDEO CAMERA we have been watching, drives down the side of the road on a pair of treads.

Across the street, an Iraqi BUTCHER wearing a bloody white smock resists being moved from his outdoor stand, which consists of little more than goat carcasses hung on metal hooks.

From all sides, American military arrive in armored TROOP
CARRIERS, disgorging teams of U.S. ARMY INFANTRY SOLDIERS who
shout "secure the area', 'watch your six,' 'stop traffic', etc.

TITLE:

BAGHDAD, 2004

This is all taking place in a densely populated, very noisy
section of Baghdad; the SOUND of far off GUNSHOTS and CALL to
prayer magnify the turmoil of a metropolis in the midst of an
occupation/insurgency/civil war.


EXT STREET DAWN

The BUTCHER, furious with the way he's being pushed around, is
forcibly removed from his shop by several IRAQI SOLDIERS.


EXT STREET DAWN - ROBOT CAM POV

Via the low-angle video camera we glimpse a herd of GOATS
scampering through frame. BURKA-clad WOMEN and OLD MEN in
traditional garb flee the scene.

Several more U.S. INFANTRY SOLDIERS move a few straggler
PEDESTRIANS away from a trash pile and the TALON ROBOT.

View momentarily blocked by STATIC INTERFERENCE.

But when the screen clears, we close in on one particular TRASH
PILE topped with a white plastic garbage bag.

Whatever it is that has everyone so afraid lies inside this bag.


EXT MIDDLE EASTERN STREET - DAWN

The TALON ROBOT pokes around the bag and the trash pile with its
mechanical VISE GRIP.


UPRANGE

Next to a parked Humvee, THREE EOD (Explosive Ordnance Disposal,
aka Bomb Squad) SOLDIERS crouch over a laptop computer screen
showing an image of the TRASH PILE.

Working the joystick on the laptop is SERGEANT J. T. SANBORN, a
type-A jock, high school football star, cocky, outgoing, ready
with a smile and quick with a joke... or, if you prefer, a jab
to the chin. Think Muhammad Ali with a rifle.

>               SANBORN
>     I think we have touchdown.

**DOWNRANGE**

The robot grinds the dirt, edging closer to the bag.

**UPRANGE**

Standing near Sanborn, SERGEANT FIRST CLASS MATT THOMPSON wipes
the sweat on his brow. Although he's the team leader, every inch
the professional soldier working a routine mission, Thompson's
normally rock-solid nerves are wavering in the punishing desert
heat.

While nibbling on a SNICKERS candy bar, Thompson glances over
his shoulder noting potential threats: a WOMAN in a VEIL and
then TWO MALES in a window - all of whom are watching him with
inscrutable expressions.

Thompson turns back to Sanborn and the task at hand:

**LAPTOP SCREEN**

We glide across the pile. Flies buzzing.

Puffs of dust and fluttering plastic.

Advancing slowly, inch by inch, to the edge for our first
glimpse *inside* the bag:

*A RUSTY ARTILLERY SHELL WITH A WIRE PROTRUDING FROM THE NOSE
CONE.*

**UPRANGE**

>               SANBORN
>     Hello mamma.

Zoom in on the nose cone of the shell.

>               THOMPSON
>          (re: the robot's camera)
>     Push it in.

>               SANBORN
>     I can't.

>           THOMPSON
> What do you mean - you can't? Pretend
> it's your dick.

>           SANBORN
> How about I pretend it's *your* dick?

>           THOMPSON
> You'll never get it in if you do that.
> Let me try.

A THIRD SOLDIER, clearly enjoying the two men he's with, leans
in for a better look. This is SPECIALIST OWEN ELDRIDGE, the
youngest of the group, impressionable, vulnerable, yet quite
capable of showing surprising backbone.

>           SANBORN
> Give me a second.

>           THOMPSON
> No. Time is up. <u>My dick</u>.

They change places.  Thompson now on the controls. They can see
protruding from the rusty shell the tell-tale wire of an
Improvised Explosive Device (IED).

>           THOMPSON
> See that?

>           SANBORN
> Nice one-five-five.

>           THOMPSON
> Yeah. That's going to do some damage.

>           SANBORN
>             (calling over his
>              shoulder)
> Hey Eldridge, we're going to need a
> charge.

Eldridge is already on it, approaching with the four blocks of
C4 plastic explosive.  He's done this enough to know what they
need.

>           ELDRIDGE
> Got it. Figured four blocks, gives you
> about twenty pounds of bang total. Are
> we going to be far enough away?

Thompson takes stock of the situation. We see the IED in the
distance -- far, far away.

                    THOMPSON
         The blast is going to roll out there
         (pointing) the shell will probably
         kick out there (pointing), and most of
         the shrapnel is going to rain up in a
         beautiful umbrella pattern. Some
         smaller pieces and shell fragments
         will come out this way but we'll be
         okay if we are behind the Humvee.
         Bring the bot back and we will load
         up.

                    SANBORN
         No problem. Bot is moving.

                                        CUT TO:


**DOWNRANGE NEAR PLASTIC BAG**

The bot dutifully makes its return voyage back to the men.


**ACROSS THE STREET**

A crowd of angry pedestrians is being held in place by a few
Iraqi soldiers, but when one soldier turns aside to help an old
man, the cantankerous BUTCHER slips past and dashes back to his
store.


**UPRANGE**

Eldridge clips a make-shift wagon to a hitch on the rear of the
robot. Inside the wagon, he's placed an array of C4. Sanborn
asks "ready?," Eldridge replies "good to go."

                    SANBORN
         Alright. Wagon is set. Bot moves.

The bot returns downrange, towing the cart and a coil of
unspooling detonation wire, which Eldridge is holding.

When...

the HERD of GOATS from earlier circles back and momentarily
impedes the robot.

                    SANBORN
                 (laughing)
         Goats! Blow those bastards up.

**DOWNRANGE**

The robot churns down the now empty street.

**UPRANGE**

Thompson scans his surroundings, finds a third IRAQI MALE watching him from a nearby balcony.

A flicker of concern flashes across his face.

**DOWNRANGE**

The robot hits a bump and a rock jams in the wagon's wheel and breaks the lock nut, popping the wheel and causing the whole rig to grind to a halt.

**UPRANGE**

Everyone cringes.

**DOWNRANGE**

The wagon is stranded.

**UPRANGE**

Sanborn wiggles the stick.  It's not happening.

> SANBORN
> Wagon is having a bad day.

> THOMPSON
> (to Eldridge)
> Did you build that?

> ELDRIDGE
> No, the U.S. Army did.

> THOMPSON
> It looks like I'm going down there.

> SANBORN
> What, you don't like waiting around
> this beautiful neighborhood?

Thompson ruefully tosses his helmet into the truck.

                    THOMPSON
          I love it.

                                        CUT TO:


**EXT  HUMVEE  MOMENTS LATER**

Sanborn unpacks "THE SUIT." A state-of-the-art contraption that
looks like an astronaut suit and helmet crossed with the
Michelin Man. Because of its weight and complexity it takes two
men to put it on - or one Sanborn.

Sanborn kneels down and guides Thompson's feet into the suit's
black boots, then lashes up a series of Velcro straps to secure
the armor, like a squire working on a knight.

Thompson twists to get his chest protector on. Eyes tight, brow
furrowed, squints into the far distance. *That's going to be a
mean motherfucker.*

                    THOMPSON
          Okay. I'm going to make my approach.
          This area looks okay. No power-lines.
          Clean line of sight. If it looks
          alright when I get down there, I'm
          going to plug it in and we'll just BIP
          it. I want them to know if they're
          going to leave a bomb on the side of
          the road, we're going to blow up their
          little fucking road.

                    SANBORN
          Ready?

                    THOMPSON
          I'm craving a hamburger, is that
          strange?

                    SANBORN
          Not for you.

Sanborn seals Thompson's helmet with a glass plate while
Eldridge attaches a breathing hose.

                    THOMPSON
                 (headset from inside the
                  helmet)
          This is Blaster One.

                         SANBORN
                    (into walkie)
               Roger that. Blaster One. You're good
               to go.

Thompson begins the lonely walk toward the bomb.

Sanborn checks on the TWO IRAQI males in the balcony by glassing
them with his M4 scope.


**SCOPE POV**

The men are smiling. Low threat.


**DOWNRANGE**

Constrained by the eighty-pound suit, sweat in his eyes,
Thompson LUMBERS down the road, emitting dust clouds with every
step.

                         THOMPSON
                    (headset)
               Nice and hot in here...
               One fifty.


**UPRANGE - HUMVEE**

                         SANBORN
                    (into walkie)
               Roger that.  A hundred and fifty
               meters.

An excited, blustering YOUNG IRAQI MALE, having just exited a
nearby building, approaches Sanborn with his hand extended in
greeting:

                         YOUNG MAN
               Hi, where are you from?

Sanborn shakes his head, raises his rifle.

The young man maintains a nervous grin.

                         SANBORN
               No.

                         YOUNG MAN
               California? New York?

Now they are standing close to each other.

                    SANBORN
      Get out of here man.

                    YOUNG MAN
      Where?

                    SANBORN
      This ain't a fucking meet-and-greet.
      GET OUT OF HERE!

Sanborn shoves the young man in the chest hard enough to nearly
knock him over.

                    SANBORN
            GO!

The man skulks away, offended and confused.

Eldridge -- who is about thirty feet away and inspecting a
burned out car -- notices this interaction out of the corner of
his eye and keys his walkie to Sanborn:

                    ELDRIDGE
      Making friends again, Sanborn?

                    SANBORN
            (smiling)
      All day long.


**DOWNRANGE**

Thompson walks on.

The desert sun glints off a nearby car and momentarily bleaches
his mask bright white.

A YOUNG GIRL with an INFANT BABY in her arms appears in a far
off doorway, then withdraws out of sight.


**UPRANGE**

Eldridge and Sanborn are at the ready, scanning the area and
watching Thompson.


**DOWNRANGE**

Thompson: careful footfalls on sand.

                    THOMPSON
               (headset)
          Twenty five.


**UPRANGE**

Sanborn wearily keys the walkie.

                    SANBORN
               (walkie)
          Roger, twenty five. You are now in the
          kill zone.

                    THOMPSON
               (headset)
          Thanks for reminding me.

Eldridge nods.  Everything progressing nice and easy.

**DOWNRANGE NEAR PLASTIC BAG**

Thompson stands over the blasting caps, picks them up and heads
for the bomb.

                    THOMPSON
               (headset)
          Dets look okay.

                    SANBORN
               (over walkie)
          Roger that.

Thompson carefully lays the C4 on top of the IED.

                    THOMPSON
               (headset)
          Laying on the charge.
               (beat) )
          Good to go, coming back.

Thompson gets up, looks around at the empty road under heavy
guard.

The war has stopped for him and he knows it.

Thompson begins to walk back uprange, looking carefully at the
ground around him.

                    THOMPSON
               (headset)
          Five meters.

                    SANBORN
                (walkie)
        Five meters, roger that.


**UPRANGE**

Sanborn and Eldridge lower their rifles.


**DOWNRANGE NEAR PLASTIC BAG**

Thompson carefully nudges a Coke can out of the way of his
boots.


**UPRANGE**

Eldridge, killing time, turns to Sanborn as they both watch
Thompson.

                    ELDRIDGE
        Hey Sanborn, you know what this place
        needs?

Looking around the war torn dirt street, the mud colored
buildings, and endless expanse of dust and sand. Nothing but
brown on brown.

                    SANBORN
        I'm listening.

                    ELDRIDGE
        Grass.

                    SANBORN
        We gonna start our grass business?

                    ELDRIDGE
        That's right. I'm going to sell the
        grass -- and you're going to cut it.
        It's going to be called 'Sanborn and
        Sons.' We'll be rich.

                    SANBORN
        I like that. Crab grass, St.
        Augustine, I'm a scholar on this shit.
        How about this? You sell it -- I
        fertilize it.

                    THOMPSON O.S.
                (headset)
        Twenty five.

>           SANBORN
>               (walkie)
>       Twenty five. Roger that.

Eldridge squints into the sun.

Out of the corner of his eye he sees movement in the butcher shop and raises his carbine.

**SCOPE POV**

The BUTCHER is holding a cell phone.

**UPRANGE**

>           ELDRIDGE
>       Hey Sanborn -- Butcher shop - two
>       o'clock! Dude has a phone!

>           SANBORN
>       Make him put it down --

Eldridge runs toward the butcher shop.

Sanborn raises his scope but Eldridge is blocking his line of fire and he can't get a shot.

>           ELDRIDGE
>           (shouting, waving his gun)
>       Hey - put that down--

The BUTCHER nods and puts up his hand as if to say, 'give me a minute.'

**DOWNRANGE**

Thompson senses trouble:

>           THOMPSON
>               (headset)
>       Why is Eldridge running? Come on guys,
>       talk to me.

**UPRANGE**

Eldridge runs hard

>           ELDRIDGE
>       *Drop the phone!*

Sanborn bolts sideways, trying to maneuver around Eldridge to a clear sight line--

                    SANBORN                          ELDRIDGE
       (shouting to Eldridge)        *PUT DOWN THE CELL PHONE!*
*Burn him! Eldridge burn him!*

Eldridge, legs pumping, flicks the rifle safety--

**BUTCHER SHOP**

The Butcher smiles. Gives Eldridge the thumbs up sign.

His other handing dials the phone.

**UPRANGE**

Sanborn sprinting but still can't find a shooting angle.

Eldridge is on fire:

                  ELDRIDGE                          SANBORN
*DROP THE PHONE!!!*                *GET OUT OF THE WAY -- BURN
                                    HIM!!*

                        ELDRIDGE
              *I CAN'T GET A SHOT!!!!*

**DOWNRANGE**

Now Thompson starts to run.  Terror in his eyes.

**ELDRIDGE SCOPE POV**

Prevented from locking aim on the butcher by two telephone polls.

**BUTCHER SHOP**

The Butcher smiles back at Eldridge

*ECU: the Butcher's eyes.*

*ECU: his thumb on send button of the cell phone.*

DOWNRANGE

Thompson running full out now when

BOOM!! --

-- A giant billowing fireball bursts from the bomb

-- flattening Thompson

-- blood splatters the inside of his helmet. Then:

-- a secondary explosion erupts

-- spewing dust and a wave of particulate matter

-- enveloping Eldridge and Sanborn *in a coarse cloud of debris.*

-- we stay on the blast's aftermath as the last dust *roils* out in slow motion and

-- floats silently over Thompson's slain body

                                            CUT TO:


**INT CAMP VICTORY  WAREHOUSE MORTUARY AFFAIRS - DAY**

An officious young MORTUARY AFFAIRS SOLDIER opens the wooden lid of a very white large box.

Inside, wrapped in plastic, are the remains of a soldier's life: a pair of boots, a toothbrush, a comb, an American flag.

Sanborn stares. Struggling to find meaning in the objects.

Now we see that he's standing in a large warehouse, the mortuary affairs office, which is filled with rows and rows of many other identical white boxes.

                    MORTUARY SOLDIER
          Anywhere is good.

Sanborn gently places Thompson's dog tags in the box.

                    SOLDIER
          Is that everything?

                    SANBORN
          Yeah.

The white box closes. Latches secure the lid.

And that's that. The soldier walks away.

Sanborn grips the box. He does not let go.

**EXT CAMP VICTORY  DAY**

Sanborn trudges across a camp clearing which is bounded by the
barracks and rows of identical aluminum trailers.

**INT TRAILER**

Inside a darkened standard-issue military trailer Ministry is
BLASTING, rattling the walls.

Sanborn knocks on the door, hears "yeah, it's open, come in,"
and steps inside.

He's greeted by a MAN holding a roofing hammer in one hand and a
cigarette in the other. This is SERGEANT FIRST CLASS WILLIAM
JAMES, his new boss.

Sanborn extends his hand and they shake.

                    SANBORN
          Sergeant James? J.T. Sanborn, my man.

                    JAMES
          Call me Will.

                    SANBORN
          Welcome to Bravo Company and welcome
          to Camp Victory.

                    JAMES
          Camp Victory? I thought this was Camp
          Liberty.

                    SANBORN
          No, they changed the name about a week
          ago. 'Victory' sounds better.

An awkward silence ensues allowing us to get a better look at
James. Though a former U.S. Army Ranger in his early thirties,
fit and good-looking, one of the lucky ones, he possesses an
unusual demeanor. In a world of outgoing young men, James seems
markedly self-absorbed. Sanborn notices this trait instantly and
is puzzled by it. The truth is that after so many years down
range, racking up kills and disarming bombs, James has lost some
of the ability and most of the need to connect to other people.

Right now, however, James is doing his best to act like a regular nice guy.

> JAMES
> Alright. Well I guess I'm in the right place.
> (Beat)
> As long as you are here, could you give me a hand with this?

James jerks his head to a window covered with a board of plywood. He walks over to it and starts removing the wood, motioning for Sanborn to grab one end of the board.

> SANBORN
> Maybe you shouldn't take this down. We get a lot of mortars at night here. The plywood helps stop the lateral frag from coming through. That's why it's up there.

> JAMES
> It's not going to stop a mortar from coming through the roof -- you know. Besides, I like the sunshine...(awkwardly) I'm sorry about Thompson, I heard he was a good tech.

> SANBORN
> Yeah, he was, and he was a great team leader too.

> JAMES
> I'm not trying to fill his shoes. I'm just going to do my best.

> SANBORN
> Appreciate it.

Although Sanborn is almost warming to his new Sergeant, James has reached his intimacy limit.

He cranks the music, grabs his still-burning cigarette, and flops down on the bed -- all in one surprisingly fluid motion.

Then announces cheerfully:

> JAMES
> Home sweet home.

                                                    CUT TO:

**INT HUMVEE CAMP VICTORY**

Sanborn is behind the wheel.  James is in the passenger seat.
Eldridge is in the back seat.

Looking through the Humvee window, we drive past a long line of
M1 Abrams battle tanks. They're neatly parked and gathering sand
on all horizontal surfaces.

>               ELDRIDGE
> Aren't you glad the Army has all these
> tanks parked here, just in case the
> Russians come and we have to have a
> big tank battle.

>               SANBORN
> I'd rather be on the side with the
> tanks, just in case.

>               ELDRIDGE
> But they don't do anything here.
> Anybody comes alongside the Humvee,
> we're dead. Anybody even looks at you
> funny, we're dead. Pretty much, the
> bottom line, is if you're in Iraq
> you're dead. How's a fucking tank
> supposed to stop that?

>               SANBORN
> Shut the fuck up, Owen.

>               ELDRIDGE
>      (smiling)
> Sorry.  Just trying to scare the new
> guy.

James shrugs this off:

>               JAMES
> I saw a little bit in Afghanistan.

**EXT  CAMP VICTORY/BAGHDAD OUTSKIRTS  MORNING**

The Humvee moves out of the base and into the outskirts of the
teeming city.

**TITLE:**

**DAYS LEFT IN BRAVO COMPANY'S ROTATION: 38**

**INT  HUMVEE**

                    SANBORN
        Hey Owen -- watch the fucking road.

The Humvee edges close to a cluster of cars. Eldridge moves up
to the gunner's seat on top of the Humvee.


**EXT  HUMVEE**

Eldridge has a collection of half-empty water bottles that he
keeps in the gunner's nest.

He throws a water bottle at the car in front of him.

It smashes into the car's rear windshield.

A passenger inside spins, enraged. He sees the Humvee. Settles
for a one finger salute for the American.

                    ELDRIDGE
        Imshee -- Imshee !


**EXT BAGHDAD STREET  EARLY MORNING**

The Humvee grinds to a stop in a ghetto overflowing with trash,
with more mud dwellings that look as beaten down as the people.

James is first out, lighting another cigarette.

Sanborn comes up behind him. Eldridge climbs out of the turret.

They are now completely out in the open, feet on Iraqi ground,
where anything can happen.

Eldridge begins turning suspicious bits of plastic over with the
tip of his boots.

                    JAMES
            (looking around at the
            empty street)
        Where are the guys who called this in?

James walks on down the street.

Sanborn and Eldridge exchange a glance 'what the hell,' and
follow him.

Meanwhile, in the background, Iraqi civilians go about their
daily life.

                    SANBORN
                 (into walkie)
          Victory Main, Victory Main, this is
          Blaster Mike. Interrogative, do you
          have an updated position?

                    DISPATCH O.S.
                 (over walkie)
          This is Victory Main. Negative.
          Figures to follow. Grid 3453.

                    SANBORN
                 (into walkie)
          Well, that's exactly where I am and I
          don't see anybody in fatigues.

                    DISPATCH O.S.
          Give me a second to confirm. That
          visual is 3453.

James, Sanborn and Eldridge continue their slow walk down the
street.

Around a corner, an empty Humvee comes into view.

                    JAMES
          We got a Humvee.

On the other side of the street, Sanborn rounds the corner,
approaching the Humvee. He shouts in case someone is inside.

                    SANBORN
          Friendly!

But there is nobody to hear him. The truck is empty.

Eldridge looks inside the vehicle, checking for blood.

James sees a tiny American flag being waved in the window of a
nearby building, and heads over to it.

                    ELDRIDGE
                 (scared)
          They abandoned their vehicle.

                    SANBORN
                 (scared too)
          We got an empty Humvee over here!

                    JAMES
          Got it!

**EXT/INT BAGHDAD BUILDING DAY**

James peers into a garden where a half dozen young SOLDIERS are resting and trying not to look afraid, and one SERGEANT CARTER is trying not to look embarrassed.

> JAMES
> Morning boys. Don't tell me the bomb
> is in there with you.

> SERGEANT CARTER
> Let's step outside, I'll show you
> what's going on.

He moves into the open and points down the block.

> SERGEANT CARTER
> Down the block, about 20 meters this
> side of the mosque, East side of the
> street, one of our informants saw
> wires in a rubble pile - possible IED.
> I trust this guy, I know him. You want
> to talk to him?

> JAMES
> I'll handle it. Keep your guys back.
>     (to Eldridge)
> Specialist! Bring up the Humvee!

Sanborn is already unloading the robot.

> SANBORN
> What's going on?

> JAMES
> Break out the suit.

> SANBORN
> What about the bot?

> JAMES
> I'll take care of it.

> SANBORN
> What? Don't you want us to get the bot
> down there to see what it looks like?

> JAMES
> I'll handle it.

> SANBORN
> It's kind of tight down here, James.

James grins. Sanborn shoots Eldridge a look. *Is he a new guy or what?*

**EXT HUMVEE   MOMENTS LATER**

Sanborn and Eldridge kneel before James, buckling on the suit.

>                    SANBORN
>          You know you don't have to go down
>          there, man, we already have the bot
>          half way out.

>                    JAMES
>          It will be alright.

Sanborn puts the helmet on.

>                    SANBORN
>          First day, I was thinking you might
>          want to take it easy.

Now enclosed in the suit, James is ready to go.

>                    JAMES
>          Let's rock 'n roll.

James heads downrange, a jaunty bounce to his step.

In stark contrast to Thompson's cautious, lumbering gait, he seems eager, almost happy, to approach the bomb.

The guys watch him go.

>                    ELDRIDGE
>          He's a rowdy boy.

>                    SANBORN
>          He's reckless.

**EXT   BAGHDAD STREET**

Without warning, James tosses a round metal canister, a smoke grenade, into the middle of the street.

**ECU:** canister jets explode, propelling a billowing cloud of gray smoke.

**EXT  HUMVEE**

Sanborn looks on in confusion as the dense smoke fills the street, obscuring his view of James.

> SANBORN
> (walkie)
> Blaster One, what's going on?

No answer. James disappears into the smoke.

> SANBORN
> (walkie)
> Blaster One, what are you doing?

No answer.

> SANBORN
> (walkie)
> Blaster one, this is Blaster Mike.
> What's with the smoke on the side of
> the road?

No answer.

> SANBORN O.S.
> (walkie)
> Hey James, can you hear me? What's
> with the smoke?

> JAMES  O.S.
> (headset)
> Creating a diversion.

Sanborn can no longer see James through the smoke.

He climbs up on top of the Humvee to get a better look. But he gets only a partial view.

> SANBORN
> (walkie)
> From what? Is there a threat?
> (to Eldridge)
> Get up on that wall. Tell me what you
> see, Specialist!

Eldridge leaps onto a nearby narrow stone wall, feet precariously balanced.

> ELDRIDGE
> I got him. He's walking downrange.

                    SANBORN
               (walkie)
     James, the smoke is killing my
     visibility. Where are you in relation
     to the IED? Are you within 100 meters,
     yet?


**EXT   BAGHDAD STREET/INTERSECTION**

                    JAMES
               (headset)
     Hell, I don't know. I'll let you know
     when I'm standing over it.

We see the world from James' point of view: the city takes on an
intense, dreamy hue as if *somehow* we're in some sort of fugue
state.

James walks on and the world returns to normal as he nears an
intersection guarded on either side by a HUMVEE and several
SOLDIERS, when...

Suddenly a red-and-white TAXI swerves past the SOLDIERS on the
left side of the intersection.

The soldiers take cover and shout contradictory commands - "Stop
the car" "Get Down Don't Move! Back up! Out of the vehicle!"

The TAXI BRAKES in front of James.


**EXT   HUMVEE**

Sanborn and Eldridge can hear the shouting but the lingering
smoke still obscures their sight.

                    ELDRIDGE
               (shouting to Sanborn)
     Car! Car! A car stopped in front of
     him.


**EXT   BAGHDAD STREET/INTERSECTION**

James' headset barks to life:

                    SANBORN O.S.
               (headset)
     James, come back *now*.

James pulls a pistol from his holster, aims it at the car...

SOLDIER

                   SOLDIER
              (over walkie)
      EOD has a nine on the Haji in the car.
      Should I send back up?

JAMES

                   JAMES
              (headset)
      I got it.

DRIVER'S FACE

Impossible to discern whether he's simply an annoyed taxi driver
-- or a Jihadi on a suicide mission.

EXT  HUMVEE

                   SANBORN
            (into walkie to soldier)
      Negative, negative. You're too close,
      the blast will come up the street.
      Stand down. Stay behind the corner.
      EOD has the situation under control.

EXT  BAGHDAD STREET/INTERSECTION

James aims at the windshield. The driver is impassive.

Soldiers shout, "get out of the car!"

James SHOOTS two rounds into the dirt near the car's front tire.

The Driver remains still.  Staring back.

James gestures with the pistol.

                   JAMES
      It's that way...Back.

James FIRES --

-- smashing the windshield into a million shards of glass.

*But the car doesn't budge.*

Now James jams his gun into the driver's forehead.

**SOLDIER**

> SOLDIER
> (into walkie)
> Three, four rounds fired. The nine is
> now pressing into the Haji's forehead.

**JAMES**

The driver slowly shifts into reverse and eases the taxi back to
the soldiers.

Soldiers rush the car, yank the driver out and pound him roughly
to the ground.

The taxi driver is zip tied and dragged away.

> JAMES
> (into mic)
> If he wasn't an insurgent he sure as
> hell is now.

**DOWNRANGE**

James resumes his walk, noting possible threats -- a MAN in a
window down the road, TWO KIDS in another window.

**EXT   BAGHDAD STREET/RUBBLE PILE IED**

One of a million in this city. James draws near. Two wires
protrude from the mess.

Moment of decision.

Moving quickly, James removes rubble and trash to expose the
wires and the artillery shells.

He kneels down into the rubble pile. Touches the bomb.

Then with great care, he removes the blasting cap from the bomb,
making sure that it doesn't make contact with the metal edges of
the artillery shell.

He cuts one wire leading to the blasting cap.

Then he flips the artillery round over and cuts the other wire.

                         JAMES
                       (headset)
              We're done. Good to go.


**UPRANGE**

                        SANBORN
              Come down, Specialist.

                        ELDRIDGE
                 Roger.

Eldridge jumps from the wall.


**DOWNRANGE**

James stands and uses his big boot to clear more rubble,
revealing: *Another wire snaking out* of the ground.

                         JAMES
                       (headset)
                 *Got a wire. Hang on..*

James traces this wire, pulling it out of the ground, inch by
inch, like extracting a buried root.

The more he pulls, the more wire gets revealed.

It doesn't seem to end.


**BALCONY**

Overhead, a YOUNG FACTORY WORKER on a high balcony studies James
as he unearths the wire.


**EXT  BAGHDAD STREET/RUBBLE PILE IED**

James, still pulling the wire, comes to a length that ends in a
bundle of wires that spider out in several different directions.

                         JAMES
                       (headset)
                 Secondary!

He pulls on this bundle and unearths a second IED.

Then he finds a third IED.

Then a fourth bomb.

Then realizes he's surrounded by a ring of IEDs.

This is the daisy-chain. One of the deadlier forms of IEDs.

**UPRANGE**

>               SANBORN
>           (to Eldridge)
>         Off the wall, Owen!
>           (to soldiers)
>       Get behind something. Find cover.

Soldiers scrambling to find concrete to hide behind.

**BALCONY**

The factory worker leaves his position and heads down the stairs.

We follow him walking down the stairs, intercut with:

James working on the bombs individually.

*ECU: James' helmet - glass clouding over from condensation -- losing visibility.*

*ECU: blasting cap*

**ECU:** feet on stairs

*ECU: knife tip separates the wire.*

**INT BUILDING STAIRCASE**

The factory worker is now on a landing, still heading down.

**EXT STREET**

James notices the worker coming down and quickens his pace.

**INT BUILDING STAIRCASE**

The worker matches James' accelerated movements, and is now rushing down the stairs.

**EXT STREET**

The worker reaches the bottom of the stairs, opens the building's front door, and steps into the street.

He looks at James.

James shows him the last blasting cap, indicating that the bombs have all been rendered safe.

The worker reveals nothing.

He turns and steps down an alley. As he goes he drops a 9-volt battery.

We find a WIRE TERMINAL attached to the alley wall, where on a different day the battery would have been connected to initiate the bomb.

CUT TO:

**EXT HUMVEE MOMENTS LATER**

James strides uprange. Eldridge isn't sure what to make of James. Sanborn is, but not ready to show it.

Sanborn unstraps the Velcro on James' bomb suit, yanking roughly. This gets James attention.

> JAMES
> That wasn't too bad, for our first time working together. What do you think?

> SANBORN
> I think working together is I talk to you. And *you* talk to me.

> JAMES
> Are we going on a date, Sanborn?

Sanborn stands face-to-face with James.

> SANBORN
> No, we're going on a mission. And it's my job to keep you safe, so we can keep going on missions.

> JAMES
> Hey, this is combat.

James pats Sanborn on the shoulder, moves to the Humvee for a
Marlborough.

Sanborn and Eldridge confer out of ear-shot.

>               ELDRIDGE
> It's just thirty nine days.

>               SANBORN
> Thirty eight. Assuming we survive
> today.

PRELAP:

Electronic GRUNTS of a first-person shooter video game.


**INT   HEAD SHED   SIDE OFFICE**

In a small recreation area, Eldridge, on a couch, plays Gears of
War on a flat screen TV.

LT. COL. JOHN CAMBRIDGE, a combat stress therapist, enters.

>               ELDRIDGE
> Hey, it's mister "Be all that you can
> be." What's up, doc?

>               CAMBRIDGE
> Not much. How are you?

>               ELDRIDGE
> I'm good. I had a question about that
> song, though. What if all I can be is
> dead on the side of an Iraqi road? I
> think it's logical. This is a war.
> People die all the time. Why not me?

>               CAMBRIDGE
> You got to stop obsessing. Change the
> record in your head. Think about other
> things. Right now, what are you
> thinking about?

>               ELDRIDGE
> You want to know what I'm thinking
> about?

>               CAMBRIDGE
> Yes.

Eldridge picks up his M4 rifle, which had been resting on the
couch, and puts his finger on the trigger.

                    ELDRIDGE
          This is what I'm thinking about.
          Here's Thompson dead.
                    (Now he dry fires. CLICK.
                    He snaps the slide back.)
          Here, he's alive.

Finger back on safe. He dry fires again.

                    ELDRIDGE
          He's dead. He's alive.


**EXT. CAMP VICTORY  MESS TENT  DAY**

Midday in Iraq. The heat is oppressive, biblical.

James is walking around the base when he's stopped by a young
Iraqi KID selling pirated DVDs.

The kid, whose name is BECKHAM, is a street savvy punk.

                    BECKHAM
          Hey, wassup my nigger? You cool or
          not? You want to buy the cool shit?
          The tight shit? No? Fuck you!
                    (he targets James)
          Hey nigger, buy some DVDs? New
          releases. Very good.

                    JAMES
          How much?

                    BECKHAM
          One for five, two for nine.

                    JAMES
                    (having fun)
          Three for twelve.

                    BECKHAM
          Three for thirteen. And for you, no
          tax.

                    JAMES
          No tax? Alright.

                    BECKHAM
          You're a smart shit, you know. You're
          not like those stupid fuck face shits.

                    JAMES
          I'm a smart guy? You're a smart kid.
          Give me your best one.

                    BECKHAM
          Here you go. This is the best shit.

James pays. Offers a cigarette.

                    JAMES
          Keep the change. Want a cigarette? Are
          you kidding? You shouldn't smoke.


**INT CAMP VICTORY  SHOWER STALLS  NEXT MORNING**

Sanborn is shaving in a mirror, otherwise dressed for combat and
ready to go.

James shuffles in wearing a T-shirt and boxer shorts, looking
like he just woke up.

James starts to brush his teeth.

                    SANBORN
          I need to talk to you about something
          before we roll out again.

                    JAMES
          Shoot.

                    SANBORN
          Yesterday -- that was not cool.

                    JAMES
          I know. You'll get it.

Sanborn wipes his face, trying to stay calm, notices a tatoo on
James' forearm.

                    SANBORN
          You were a Ranger? I was in
          intelligence seven years before EOD.
          We ran combat missions in every shit
          hole on the planet.
               (beat)
          So I'm pretty sure I can figure out a
          redneck piece of trailer trash like
          you.

James grins.

                    JAMES
          Looks like you're on the right track.


**INT/EXT HUMVEE   UNITED NATIONS TEMPORARY HEADQUARTERS MORNING**

The men drive into a parking lot teeming with people on the run,
hundreds of UN EMPLOYEES, mostly white, many dressed in business
suits, flee the United Nations building.

Parked beside the building is a <u>blue sedan</u>.

**TITLE OVER:**

**DAYS LEFT IN BRAVO COMPANY'S ROTATION: 37**

The Humvee passes through a roadblock, stops, and James gets out
to talk to an IRAQI SERGEANT.

Due to his current position in the parking lot, James can't see
the blue sedan that everyone is running from.

                    IRAQI SERGEANT
          It's behind the wall.

                    JAMES
          Did you see any wires? Any smoke?

                    IRAQI SERGEANT
          No. I didn't look.

                    JAMES
          So how do you know it's a bomb?

                    IRAQI SERGEANT
          The car has been parked there
          illegally and the suspension is
          sagging, so there's definitely
          something heavy in the trunk.

                    JAMES
          Why don't you peek inside and tell me
          what you see?

                    IRAQI SERGEANT
          You want me to go close to it? In
          Arabic: you crazy piece of shit!

                                        CUT TO:

**EXT  UN BUILDING  NEAR SEDAN  MOMENTS LATER**

James now dressed in the bomb suit walks beside the Humvee towards the blue sedan.

Workers continue to stream out of the building, hurrying faster down a flight of stairs when they see James in the bomb suit.

James comes to within twenty feet of the blue sedan. He stops.

**BALCONY**

On a third-floor balcony, unseen by the soldiers, a INSURGENT SNIPER takes aim.

**SEDAN**

-- a SHOT rings out

-- bullet strikes the car

-- it bursts into flames

-- a plume of flame rushes out from the gas tank, like a blowtorch

-- we see the flames through James' helmet.

**EXT  STREET NEAR UN BUILDING**

"It's coming from over here", shout INFANTRY on the grounds outside the building as they FIRE M4s at the sniper's balcony.

Their bullets hit concrete, missing the sniper. A TEAM of SOLDIERS charges inside the building.

**SEDAN**

James backs away from the fire, toward Sanborn who is now running toward him with a fire extinguisher. Eldridge follows just behind Sanborn.

**EXT  UN BUILDING  PARKING LOT**

Sanborn passes James a fire-extinguisher to James.

                    ELDRIDGE
          I got top cover!

                    JAMES
          That's a negative, Specialist.
          Eldridge stay with me. Sanborn, you
          take top cover.

It takes Sanborn an instant to process the insult: top cover, in
this case, is the junior man's job.

Shaking his head, Sanborn runs to the building.

Eldridge positions himself at the top of a staircase, hunkered
down behind a low concrete wall.


**JAMES**

James sprays the extinguisher into the roaring fire. Flames lick
his suit.


**SANBORN**

Sanborn pounds up a long flight of stairs.


**JAMES**

Gaining control of the fire.


**SANBORN**

Charges through the rooftop door and runs to the edge of the
roof.


**JAMES**

The fire is nearly out, the car a smoking ruin, dusted with
white fire retardant powder.


**SANBORN**

At the edge of the roof, looking down over James and Eldridge.

                    SANBORN
                (walkie)
          Blaster Mike in position.

**INT SEDAN**

James stops. He's done. The fire is out.

He looks up at Sanborn, nods.

Then he wipes the car's blackened window and looks inside for the bad news.

**SANBORN**

Scans his surrounding, noting potential threats in every direction.

**EXT HUMVEE/STREET**

A salty officer, COLONEL REED, whose uniform shimmers with military bling and Army skill patches, crosses the street to a spot where an Army medic is treating the now badly wounded SNIPER.

Other SOLDIERS in Reed's troop stand nearby.

>                     REED
>                 (to medic)
>         What have you got?

>                     MEDIC
>         Through and through to the chest but I
>         got him stable.

>                 COLONEL REED
>                 (smiling)
>         He's not going to make it.

>                     MEDIC
>         If we're leaving in fifteen minutes we
>         got a survivable wound, Sir.

>                 COLONEL REED
>                 (giving an order to
>                 Soldier 1)
>         He's not going to make it.

The Colonel turns away. Soldiers crowd around the MEDIC, blocking our view.

We HEAR TWO SHOTS, killing the sniper –

CUT TO:

**ROOF**

The shots echo on the roof. Sanborn spins. Looks down to James.

**EXT  SEDAN**

James tries to use a crow bar to pry open the trunk but that
fails.

So he kicks the trunk with the bar, smashing it, until finally
it squeaks open, revealing...

a trunk full of South African 155 rounds, linked with det cord.

James is so taken aback that he drops the crowbar.

Then he pulls the bomb suit's quick release tab. The bomb suit
falls away.

Then he takes off his helmet.

**EXT   UN BUILDING ROOF**

>                     SANBORN
>                   (into walkie)
>             What is he doing?

**EXT   UN BUILDING  PARKING LOT**

>                     ELDRIDGE
>                   (into walkie)
>             I don't know.

**EXT  SEDAN**

>                     ELDRIDGE
>             What are you doing?

>                     JAMES
>             There's enough bang in here to send us
>             all to Jesus. If I'm going to die, I
>             want to die comfortable.

James passes the helmet to Eldridge.

>                     JAMES
>             I need my kit and my cans.

**EXT UN BUILDING ROOF**

Sanborn stares down at James and the car.  *Great.*

> SANBORN
> (into walkie)
> What's going on?

> ELDRIDGE
> (into walkie)
> I'm getting his kit and cans. (beat)
> Cover me, please.

Eldridge runs to get the equipment, while James finishes removing his suit.

Sanborn watches all this.

Across the street, a young IRAQI MAN with <u>a consumer VIDEO CAMERA is also watching.</u> He goes unnoticed.

Eldridge returns with the kit, hands it to James. James approaches the car and shines his flashlight into the trunk.

Smoke. Wires. Bombs.

> JAMES
> (into mic)
> Got a lot of det cord. Electrical.

He snips a wire.

> JAMES
> (into mic)
> I'm going to look for the initiator.

SANBORN

Nods, feeling vulnerable and exposed on the roof.

JAMES

James gets into the back seat, presses the upholstery.

> JAMES
> (into mic)
> It's not in the back seat, I don't
> think.

He rips the upholstery with his knife. Tearing out foam. But no wires.

                         JAMES
                    (into mic)
               Nope. It's not in the back seat.


**EXT  UN BUILDING ROOF**

Sanborn sees a YOUNG MAN on a balcony at 9 o'clock and waves to
him while slightly raising his rife.

The boy waves back.

                         SANBORN
                    (into walkie)
               I've got eyes on a young man on a
               balcony, at your 9 o'clock. Keep an
               eye on him.


**EXT  UN BUILDING  PARKING LOT**

Below, Eldridge raises his hand "roger that" - understood - and
nervously scans the surrounding buildings.


**INT SEDAN**

James in the front seat now rips apart the door, rips the
weather stripping to just bare metal.

                         JAMES
                    (into mic)
               It's not in the front seat... It's not
               in the door...not in the floors...not
               in the glovebox.


**EXT UN BUILDING  ROOF**

                         SANBORN
                    (into walkie)
               If you haven't found it yet it's
               probably under the car somewhere.


**INT  SEDAN**

                         JAMES
                    (headset)
               None of the cord goes under. It's up
               here -- somewhere.

**EXT UN BUILDING  ROOF**

Sanborn keeps moving to avoid being a static target. Not liking this.

**EXT UN BUILDING PARKING LOT**

Eldridge now notices the MAN on a roof-top his 12 o'clock, holding the <u>video camera</u>.

>                ELDRIDGE
>           (into walkie)
>      You got eyes on a guy with a video
>      camera?

>                SANBORN O.S.
>           (over walkie)
>      No. Where?

>                ELDRIDGE
>           (into walkie)
>      He's right at my 12 o'clock. You see
>      him? He's pointing the thing right at
>      me!

**JAMES**

Jabbing his knife into the upholstery.

**EXT UN BUILDING  ROOF**

>                SANBORN
>           (into walkie)
>      Negative. I don't see him.

**EXT  UN BUILDING PARKING LOT**

Eldridge raises his rifle, motions for the man to leave.

The man ignores him, keeps filming.

Eldridge flips.

>                ELDRIDGE
>      Right at my 12 - look 12 o'clock!

**EXT   UN BUILDING ROOF**

Sanborn jogs over to the side of the roof where he can now see the MAN that Eldridge is referring to.

> SANBORN
> (into walkie)
> Roger that, I got him. Yeah, he's shady.

**EXT   UN BUILDING   PARKING LOT**

Eldridge lifting his gun.

> ELDRIDGE
> (into walkie)
> So what's the play?

> SANBORN O.S.
> (over walkie)
> Be smart. Make a good decision.

Off Eldridge's panic:

> CUT TO:

**JAMES**

Ripping wires in the car, increasingly frustrated, sotto voice "more wires going nowhere."

> SANBORN O.S.
> (over walkie)
> Hey James, how you doing?

> JAMES
> (into mic)
> I'm wonderful. How are you?

**EXT UN BUILDING ROOF**

More and more, FACES are appearing in the windows around Sanborn and Eldridge.

> SANBORN
> (into walkie)
> We've been here a while. We need to get out of here soon. We got a lot of eyes on us.

**INT SEDAN**

James ignores this. He's in a flow state, the athlete totally
focused on the game.

He retraces what's left of the wire yet again. Thinking.

> SANBORN O.S.
> (over walkie)
> We got to get out of here.

> JAMES
> (headset)
> Roger that. I'm going to figure this
> out.

> SANBORN O.S.
> James, we need to get out of here.

James ignores him.

> SANBORN O.S.
> James do you copy?

James throws his headset walkie talkie out of the car.

It lands with a rattle on the ground.

**EXT  UN BUILDING  PARKING LOT**

> ELDRIDGE
> (into walkie)
> I'm a sitting duck.

**EXT  UN BUILDING  ROOF**

Sanborn sees below a SOLDIER helping an older woman out of the
building. The soldier looks up to Sanborn and gives him a thumbs
up sign.

> SANBORN
> How's it looking down there?

> SOLDIER
> All clear.

> SANBORN
> (into walkie)
> The building is evacuated.
> (MORE)

> SANBORN (cont'd)
> We can leave, let the engineers handle
> this mess.

**EXT   UN BUILDING   PARKING LOT**

> ELDRIDGE
> (into walkie)
> Are we moving?

**EXT   UN BUILDING   ROOF**

> SANBORN
> (into walkie)
> That's affirmative.

**SEDAN**

James pulls out the car radio.

Suddenly --

The car's rain wipers SCREECH and flap across the windshield.

> JAMES
> (sotto voce)
> Interesting.

**ROOF**

> SANBORN
> What's going on with James. He's not
> answering me.

**PARKING LOT**

> ELDRIDGE
> I think he removed his headset.

**ROOF**

> SANBORN
> (into walkie to Eldridge)
> Will you tell him to his radio back
> on.

**EXT  UN BUILDING  PARKING LOT**

>                    ELDRIDGE
>               (shouting to James)
>     Hey James, Sergeant Sanborn  is asking
>     if you'll please put your headset back
>     on.

James raises his hand and gives Eldridge the middle-finger 'fuck-you'.

>                    ELDRIDGE (CONT'D)
>               (into walkie to Sanborn)
>     That's a negative. It's not happening.

**EXT UN BUILDING  ROOF**

Sanborn is pacing now, like a caged lion.

He notices three MEN at a minaret behind him and waves to them.

>                    SANBORN
>     I got eyes on three guys at the
>     minaret. Six o'clock.

**INT SEDAN**

James keeps working. He gets out, checks under the hood of the car. Traces the wires there.

**EXT UN ROOF/PARKING LOT**

>                    SANBORN
>     What the hell is he doing?

>                    ELDRIDGE
>     I don't know - it looks like he's
>     checking the oil.

**SEDAN**

James pulls a wire. The windshield wipers stop their horrible screeching.

He goes back inside the car, checking under the steering wheel.

**EXT  UN BUILDING  ROOF**

The angry MAN in the minaret that didn't wave is now joined by two other MEN, and they begin to point to Sanborn, and then down to James and Eldridge.

They wave to the VIDEO CAMERA MAN. He waves back to them.

>           SANBORN
>       (into walkie)
>   They're communicating with your camera
>   man.

**EXT UN BUILDING  PARKING LOT**

>           ELDRIDGE
>       (into walkie)
>   This is bad.

>           SANBORN O.S.
>       (into walkie)
>   Get behind a Jersey barrier.

**EXT  UN BUILDING  PARKING LOT**

>           ELDRIDGE
>       (into walkie)
>   I can't keep eyes on James from here.

Eldridge stands.

>           SANBORN O.S.
>       (over walkie)
>   Get down. *Now.*

Eldridge crouches back down. Not sure what's right or wrong anymore.

>           ELDRIDGE
>       (to James)
>   We can go!

**INT SEDAN**

James ignores Eldridge and continues to work. Finally, he finds what he's looking for under a tangle of wires: a black box.

Slowly prying off the lid, taking it apart.

Then he throws the black box. It goes flying out of the car.

James gets out. Shouts to Eldridge.

> JAMES
> We're done... Sanborn, let's get out
> of here!

He picks up his headset, waves to Sanborn to come down off the roof.

**EXT   UN BUILDING   ROOF**

Sanborn bangs open the door to the staircase.

**EXT   UN BUILDING   PARKING LOT   MOMENTS LATER**

James is flushed, red, sweat dripping as he approaches the Humvee, a big satisfied grin on his face.

Sanborn, furious, charges him.

**INT   UN BUILDING   HUMVEE   MOMENTS LATER**

James gets inside the vehicle, lights up a cigarette.

> JAMES
> That was good.

Sanborn leans into the window.

> SANBORN
> Hey, James.

> JAMES
> Yeah?

Sanborn JABS him in the jaw, knocking the cigarette out.

> SANBORN
> Never turn your headset off again.

Sanborn stalks off and James explodes out of the car.

He crouches down, searching the floor of the Humvee. Sees his cigarette, cleans it off, then goes back to his smoke.

Once again, calm as can be, looking at Sanborn, considering him.

As James puffs away, watching Sanborn, two HUMVEE's drive down the ramp to the parking area of the building.

Several soldiers exit, among them is COLONEL REED.  SOLDIERS trot along beside him.

The Colonel strides up to Eldridge.

> COLONEL REED
> You the guy in the bomb suit?

> ELDRIDGE
> No, Sir. That's Sergeant James. He's right here.
> (to James)
> Somebody here to see you.

James comes around.

> JAMES
> Hello, sir.

> COLONEL REED
> (to James, pointing)
> You the guy in the flaming car?
> Sergeant James?

> JAMES
> Yes, sir.

> COLONEL REED
> Well, that's just hot shit. You're a wild man, you know that?

The Colonel spins his head around to an aide.

> COLONEL REED
> He's a wild man, you know that?
> (back to James)
> Let me shake your hand.

> JAMES
> Thank you, sir.

> COLONEL REED
> How many bombs have you disarmed, Sergeant?

> JAMES
> I'm not quite sure.

> COLONEL REED
> Sergeant, I asked you a question.

                    JAMES
One hundred and seventy three.
Counting today, Sir.

                    COLONEL REED
One hundred and seventy three? That
must be a record. So tell me, what's
the best way to go about disarming one
of these things?

                    JAMES
The way you don't die.

                    COLONEL REED
Good one. Spoken like a wild man.
That's good.

                                        CUT TO:


**EXT CAMP VICTORY  FIRST SERGEANT'S TRAILER  AFTERNOON**

James, sitting on a bench under a camo net, grabs a smoke and
inspects a circuit board.

A soccer ball rolls beside him.

James picks it up. The DVD kid, Beckham, comes up to retrieve
the ball.

                    BECKHAM
Give it.

                    JAMES
Wait a minute. Look who it is. I want
my five bucks back, buddy.

                    BECKHAM
Five dollars - for what? Are you
crazy?

                    JAMES
Those DVDs you sold me were crap.

                    BECKHAM
No, you're crazy. That's impossible.
It's Hollywood special effects.

                    JAMES
It was shaky and out of focus, buddy.

                    BECKHAM
          Special effects! What do you want,
          donkey porn? Girls on dog? Just tell
          me what you want! Are you gay? You
          want gay sex?

The boy's chutzpa amuses James. He's starting to like this kid.

                    JAMES
          What's your name anyway?

                    BECKHAM
          Beckham.

                    JAMES
          Oh yeah - like the soccer player? You
          good like him, too?

                    BECKHAM
          Better, my man.

James gets up. Motions for the kid to give him space.

                    JAMES
          Alright, make you a deal. If you can
          stop the ball I'll give you five bucks
          --

                    BECKHAM
          -- Five dollars? More like ten,
          twenty.

                    JAMES
          But if you can't, I'm going keep the
          ball. Deal?

                    BECKHAM
          Deal.

The boy runs to a makeshift goal post. James prepares to kick

                    JAMES
          Ready? One, two --

He kicks the ball in Beckham's direction and it flies up but
Beckham blocks it easily. He's very skillful.

                    JAMES
          -- three. Shit.

Beckham comes back over to James, ball in hand, and notices the
bomb patch on James' uniform.

                    BECKHAM
               (pointing to the patch)
          Come on, where's the five dollars. You
          are EOD. EOD -- boomala boomala. It's
          fun, no? It's gangsta?

James is surprised by the question. Not sure how to reply.


                    JAMES
          Yeah I think so. Tell you what, kid,
          I'll buy another DVD but if it's shaky
          or out of focus or in any way not 100
          percent, I'm going to chop off your
          head with a dull knife.
               (long beat)
          I'm kidding.

James affectionately puts the kid in a headlock.


**INT CAMP VICTORY  GARAGE**

Eldridge is repairing something near the under carriage of the
HUMVEE when the psychiatrist approaches.

                    CAMBRIDGE
          How's it going?

                    EDLDRIDGE
          Good. Breaks are squeaky.

                    CAMBRIDGE
          How you doing?

                    ELDRIDGE
          Good. Sleep is good. Eating well.
          Feeling pretty squared away.

                    CAMBRIDGE
          Glad to hear it. You getting along
          with the men in your unit?

                    ELDRIDGE
          Yeah, my team is great. My team leader
          is inspiring.

                    CAMBRIDGE
          You being sarcastic, soldier?

                    ELDRIDGE
          No. I mean, he's going to get me
          killed. I almost died yesterday.
               (MORE)

ELDRIDGE (cont'd)
But at least I'll die in the line of
duty, 'Proud and Strong.'

CAMBRIDGE
You know, this doesn't have to be a
bad time in your life. <u>Going to war is
a once in a life time experience. It
can be fun.</u>

ELDRIDGE
And you know this from your extensive
work in the field?

CAMBRIDGE
I've done my field duty.

ELDRIDGE
Where was that - Yale?

CAMBRIDGE
Look, if you want to stop talking to
me, you can. These sessions are
voluntary.

Eldridge considers this.

ELDRIDGE
I appreciate what you're saying. But
you need to get out from behind the
wire. See what we do.

CAMBRIDGE
If the circumstance calls for it, I
will. Just like any other soldier.

CUT TO:

**EXT BAGHDAD PURGATORY DAY**

We're at the south end of an EXPLOSIVES DISPOSAL RANGE,
nicknamed, 'Purgatory' -- an empty expanse of dirt pockmarked
with craters.

**TITLE OVER:**

**DAYS LEFT IN BRAVO COMPANY'S ROTATION: 17**

**BOOM!!!**

A tremendous EXPLOSION, by far the largest we've seen yet, kicks
out a mushroom cloud of debris.

We move across the field with the cloud and settle where our EOD
team is positioned by their Humvee.

Sanborn has a remote detonator in his hand and is about to
trigger it a second time.

>                    SANBORN
>          Ready for second det? Fire in the
>          hole. Fire in the hole.

James cheerfully interrupts --

>                    JAMES
>          Hold on a second. I think I forgot my
>          gloves back there.

James jumps into the Humvee and drives down range, reversing the
course we just took.

It's a long way to the explosives, at least half a mile.

Sanborn and Eldridge watch him recede in the distance.

James is a tiny figure ambling around the explosives pile.

Sanborn looks down at the detonator in his hand. Eldridge
notices the look.

>                    SANBORN
>                 (re detonator)
>          Those detonators misfire all the time.

>                    ELDRIDGE
>          What are you doing?

>                    SANBORN
>          I'm just saying, shit happens. They
>          misfire.

>                    ELDRIDGE
>          He'd be obliterated to nothing.

>                    SANBORN
>          His helmet would be left, you could
>          have that. Little specs of hair
>          charred on the inside.

>                    ELDRIDGE
>          Yeah, there would be half a helmet
>          somewhere...specs of hair.

> SANBORN
> We'd have to ask for change in
> technique and protocol - make sure
> this type of accident never happens
> again. You'd have to write the report.

> ELDRIDGE
> Are you serious?

> SANBORN
> I can't write it.

> ELDRIDGE
> No, are you serious about killing him?

Sanborn stares at Eldridge. Dead serious.

They look downrange at the their leader/tormentor.

He's recovered his gloves. He's celebrating that fact by pumping his fists in the air.

> CUT TO:

**INT/ EXT HUMVEE DAY**

Find the Humvee driving across the desert void. Driving and driving.

Outside, horizon of sand and sun.

Inside, shell-shocked men.

**EXT HUMVEE DAY**

The Humvee crests a hill and comes in range of a HEAVILY ARMED MAN/face wrapped in a KEFFYIEH/nationality unclear, who is waving an AK-47.

Behind him are four additional ARMED MEN of uncertain nationality, as well as a large, disabled SUV.

**INT HUMVEE**

In the turret, Eldridge fingers the trigger of his .50 machine gun.

|                                          |                                     |
|------------------------------------------|-------------------------------------|
| ELDRIDGE                                 | SANBORN                             |
| (shouting below)                         | Roger that.                         |
| 12 o'clock. I see an SUV. I              |                                     |
| got four armed men. They're in           |                                     |
| Haji gear.                               |                                     |

|                                          |                                     |
|------------------------------------------|-------------------------------------|
| JAMES                                    | SANBORN                             |
| Careful now, guys.                       | (to James)                          |
|                                          | We're in it now.                    |

                    JAMES
          Eldridge, stay on that fifty.


**EXT HUMVEE**

The keffiyeh-clad man stops waving his arms, and walks towards
the HUMVEE. Sanborn brakes.

James and Sanborn charge out of the vehicle, blood boiling, guns
high, yelling: DROP YOUR FUCKING GUNS! HANDS UP! ON YOUR KNEES!

The keffiyeh man does not comply. Instead, he shouts a reply
that is drowned out by the desert wind.

                    SANBORN
          Hands high!

                    JAMES
          Eldridge, cover!

                    ELDRIDGE
          I got you!

Sanborn continues shouting orders: GET DOWN NOW! ON YOUR KNEES
MOTHERFUCKER! HANDS ON YOUR HEAD! HANDS ON YOUR HEAD!

Finally, the keffiyeh man nods to his men, who lower their
prodigious weapons.

Then he takes his own piece...and carefully unsnaps it from the
shoulder sling.

He kneels and interlaces his hands on his head.

As James and Eldridge provide cover, Sanborn rushes forward,
shaking with adrenaline, M4 darting back and forth.

When he's close, Sanborn notices a pistol still strapped to the
man's leg.

                    SANBORN
          Pistol - take it off now.

                         KEFFIYEH MAN
                    (in English)
               What do you want me to do, put my
               hands up or take off my pistol?


                         SANBORN
               Keep your hands up.


                         KEFFIYEH MAN
               Okay.


Sanborn reaches for his pistol. It catches in the holster, then
comes free.


                         KEFFIYEH MAN
               Can I touch my fucking head now?


                         SANBORN
                    Slowly.


Slowly unfurling his Keffiyeh...


Until we see that he's not at all Arabic but just a darkly
tanned, bearded Anglo-Saxon: a former member of the British SAS
turned MERCENARY TEAM LEADER -- who at this moment is feeling
pretty sick of American yahoos.


                         MERCENARY TEAM LEADER
               We're on the same side. You guys are
               wired tight - you know that?


                         JAMES
               What are you doing out here? This is
               no place for a picnic.


                         MERCENARY TEAM LEADER
               We've got a flat tire. Can you help
               us?


                         JAMES
               Sure. Do you have spares?


                         MERCENARY TEAM LEADER
               We have a spare but we used up our
               wrench.


                         JAMES
               How do you use up a wrench?


                         MERCENARY TEAM LEADER
                    (pointing to FEISAL, one
                     of the mercenaries)
               That guy - he threw it at someone.

                    SANBORN
                (to FEISAL)
You know you don't have to throw
wrenches. You can shoot people here.

                    FEISAL
        Fuck off.

They walk back to the contractor's vehicle, where two ENEMY
PRISONERS OF WAR (EPWs, or so we assume), shrouded in black
hoods, hands bound, are kneeling uncomfortably on the desert
floor.

                                        CUT TO:


**EXT  ROAD  MOMENTS LATER**

A moment of calm:

FEISAL crouches by the SUV's flat tire, twisting a wrench.

A second mercenary - call him JIMMY - gives a drink of water to
the two bound and hooded EPWs.

The two remaining mercenaries, CHRIS and CHARLIE, quietly stand
guard around the perimeter of the SUV.

Sanborn relieves his bladder on an innocent sand dune.

James and Eldridge are hanging out with the MERCENARY TEAM
LEADER. He's bragging about his two high-value prisoners, who
appear in a DECK of MOST WANTED PLAYING CARDS.

                MERCENARY TEAM LEADER
                (re: the EPW's)
        Picked them up in Najaf. Nine of
        hearts... Jack of Clubs.

                    ELDRIDGE
        Same guys?

                MERCENARY TEAM LEADER
        That's them.

James, mildly impressed, notices that Feisal is having an issue
with the tire wrench.

            JAMES                      MERCENARY TEAM LEADER
Need a little help there?      What's the problem with the
                               tire? Why the delay?

                        FEISAL
          No good, boss. This wrench is too
          small.

                    MERCENARY TEAM LEADER
          Alright, solutions anyone?

                        ELDRIDGE
          I think there is another wrench in the
          back of the Humvee if you want to
          check.

                        FEISAL
          Thanks, I'll look.

Feisal walks to the EOD HUMVEE.

                    MERCENARY TEAM LEADER
          How long are you guys out here?

                        JAMES
          I don't know. Specialist, what do we
          got?

                        ELDRIDGE
          We've got...ah...seventeen more days.

                        JAMES
          But no one is counting, right.

Feisal returns with a new wrench, when...

--A BULLET RIPS INTO HIS BACK

--FLATTENING HIM INSTANTLY

                    MERCENARY TEAM LEADER
               *Contact left! Contact left!*

--<u>THE MERCENARIES AND SOLDIERS ALL BEGIN SHOOTING TOWARDS THEIR
LEFT HAND SIDE, UNLEASHING A BARRAGE OF INDISCRIMINATE GUNFIRE
INTO THE DESERT</u>

--ANOTHER BULLET ZIPS BY, NARROWLY MISSING ONE OF THE
CONTRACTORS.

Bedlam: as the firing continues on all sides, the mercenaries
scramble for supplies and ammunition in their SUV, following the
commands of their leader who shouts "Jimmy get the go-bags,"
"Charlie, grab the Barrett", "Chris take the fifty", "into the
ravine", etc.

CHRIS leaps into the HUMVEE turret and sprays bullets in all directions.

The soldiers dash for cover into

**EXT RAVINE**

a nearby ravine, and continue firing indiscriminately

**HUMVEE**

Chris makes the big gun smoke.

Spent brass spins red hot out of the barrel and large caliber bullets pound the desert.

But there is no enemy in sight.

**RAVINE**

> ELDRIDGE
> (shouting)
> What are we shooting at?

> SANBORN
> (shouting back)
> I don't know!

**SUV**

In the confusion, the two hooded prisoners rise up and run blindly into the desert.

**RAVINE**

Seeing that his valuable prisoners are escaping, the TEAM LEADER shouts:

> MERCENARY TEAM LEADER
> The packages are moving!

> JIMMY
> They will not get far on foot.

> MERCENARY TEAM LEADER
> Three bloody months hunting those fuckers. I'm out five hundred thousand quid!

With that, the TEAM LEADER brazenly dashes into the open in order to get an angle on the fleeing prisoners and as bullets snap around him he shoots the prisoners in the back.

Then he bolts to the ravine, very pleased with himself:

> MERCENARY TEAM LEADER (CONT'D)
> I forgot, it's five hundred thousand
> DEAD OR ALIVE!

## EXT  ROAD

Chris in the turret of the Humvee keeps firing the machine gun in all directions.

## EXT/INT  DEEP RAVINE

As the shooting continues, the Mercenary Team Leader scrambles up one side of the ravine.

> MERCENARY TEAM LEADER
> Jimmy, give me the Barrett.

[referring to a .50 caliber tripod-mounted sniper rifle]

The Mercenary Team Leader hoists this heavy gun to the edge of the ravine and looks down the scope.

Jimmy crawls next to him with a spotting scope in hand.

## EXT  ROAD

Chris is still working the machine gun, expending hundreds of bullets a minute.

## EXT/INT  DEEP RAVINE

The Mercenary Leader says to Jimmy:

> MERCENARY TEAM LEADER
> Chris is shooting wild. We have to
> conserve ammo.

> JIMMY
> (into radio)
> Hey Chris - can you hear me? Chill out
> on the fifty.

**EXT  ROAD**

Chris ceases fire for a moment and takes his finger off the
trigger. Silence while he keys his walkie.

>                    CHRIS
>               (into walkie)
>          Roger that.

-- A bullet strikes him in the neck, killing him instantly.

**EXT/INT  DEEP RAVINE**

>                    JIMMY
>          He shot Chris.

The mercenary team leader deflates. He rests his chin on the
rifle.

Everyone else in the ravine ceases firing as the futility of
their situation sinks in.

**SCOPE POV**

Scanning the barren landscape. Gravel and sun. No enemy, not a
living soul in sight.

Then...a structure...a one-story building, in the far distance.

**RAVINE**

>                    JIMMY
>          It must be coming from that building.

>                    MERCENARY TEAM LEADER
>          I can't see anything.

**SCOPE POV**

Heat shimmers.

Then...on the roof of the building...slight movement.

Possibly, it's a MAN lying prone. Possibly, it's two MEN.

**RAVINE**

>           JIMMY
> Movement on the roof.

The mercenary team leader concentrates his aim. He fires.

**BUILDING**

A pause while the bullet closes the gap - then SMASHES into the building's side, tearing apart bricks and mortar.

The figures on the roof, if they are men, have certainly gone unharmed.

**RAVINE**

>           JIMMY
> Three meters higher.

>           MERCENARY TEAM LEADER
> I've got to adjust.

He jostles the heavy sniper rifle forward a few inches.

**INT. BUILDING**

Inside the building, an INSURGENT SNIPER team peers at the ridge-ravine complex where the mercenaries and soldiers have taken cover.

**SNIPER POV**

The wispy form of the two mercenaries lying on the ridge can be faintly seen.

**INT. BUILDING**

The sniper's muzzle FLASHES.

**RIDGE**

The mercenary team leader hoists himself up into a low crawl only to --

--*take the bullet square in the chest*

--spinning him off the ridge

-- face first into the ravine

-- his back a pulped and bloody mess from the exit wound.


**RAVINE**

Jimmy jumps down from the ridge to check for a pulse.

>                    JIMMY
>          He's dead.

Now the men plummet into a full-bore panic and everyone starts
talking at once.

>          SANBORN                        JAMES
> I'll get on the Barret.          Go, go.

>          ELDRIDGE                        JAMES
> No Sanborn don't do that.        Go, go. Stay low.

>      OLDER CONTRACTOR                DISPATCH (O.S.)
>    (into radio) )               Roger that, Alpha Nine. Go
> This is Alpha Nine. We're in    ahead.
> deep shit. We're taking
> incoming fire.


**RIDGE**

Sanborn crawls to the Barrett, followed by James, who takes
Jimmy's spotting scope. Effectively, our soldiers have replaced
the first sniping team.


**RAVINE**

>                    JIMMY
>               (into walkie)
>          We are taking incoming fire. I have
>          two KIA. Correction three KIA. Can you
>          get us some help?

>                    DISPATCH (O.S.)
>          Roger that Alpha Nine. Go ahead.

>                    OLDER CONTRACTOR
>          Our grid -- MDRF:5542973420.

                          DISPATCH O.S.
                Alpha Nine, this is Big North Seven.
                You are going to have to sit tight.

Off his despair:

                                                        CUT TO:


**RIDGE**

Sanborn prepares to shoot at the men in the building.

                          JAMES
                     (quietly)
                Breathe easy. I got movement at that
                house. 800 meters. By the window: you
                have a target

                          SANBORN
                Got it.

Sanborn squeezes the trigger. The muzzle flashes.


**SCOPE POV**

A bullet strikes the left side of the house. Another miss.


**RIDGE**

                          JAMES
                     (softly)
                A little left.

Sanborn squeezes the trigger... only to hear the METALLIC CLICK
of an empty chamber.

                          SANBORN
                I'm out of ammo.

                          JAMES
                Huh?

                          SANBORN
                I'm out of ammo.

                          JAMES
                     (shouting over his
                      shoulder)
                Eldridge! We need ammo.

**RAVINE**

Eldridge frantically searches a few nearby backpacks.

**RIDGE**

>                    JAMES
>          I need that ammo man!

**RAVINE**

>                  ELDRIDGE
>          I'm looking. Where is it?
>
>                JAMES O.S.
>          Check the dead guy.

Eldridge flips over the body of the slain contractor. His chest is pulped.

Nestled in the gore are several .50 magazines. Eldridge grabs them with shaky hands and passes them up to James.

**RIDGE**

James passes the ammo to Sanborn. He slams it into the receiver.

>                    JAMES
>          Same target.
>
>                  SANBORN
>          Got it.

Sanborn pulls the trigger. Click.

**ECU:** Hand cycling the weapon. Finger pulling trigger. Bolt catching, jammed.

>                  SANBORN
>          It's jammed. The blood is making it
>          jam.

Sanborn removes the clip and hands it back to James who hands it back down to Eldridge in the ravine, instructing him:

>                    JAMES
>          Eldridge, you got to <u>clean the blood
>          off the bullets</u>. The blood is making
>          it jam.

Eldridge takes the magazine and rubs the top bullet to no good effect, for the dust on his hands sticks to the blood and the blood sticks to the bullet.

He rubs harder, only making it dirtier.

James peers down and realizes that Eldridge is lost.

> JAMES
> Spit and rub, man. Spit on them.

Eldridge tries to spit on the bullets.

His mouth is too dry to produce salvia.

He tries again. Nothing.

James sees his escalating despair and slides down the ridge, coming next to Eldridge.

> JAMES
> Use your camel (referring to the
> Camelback water canteen).

James squeezes the nipple of Eldridge's Camel and directs the water to drip on the bullets. It sort of works.

Sitting side by side now, they rub away the grime and polish the bullets to a bright shine.

> JAMES
> You're doing good, man. You're okay.
> I'm going to keep you safe.

James takes the clean bullets and climbs back to the ridge, telling Eldridge:

> JAMES
> Scan your sectors.

**RIDGE**

Sanborn loads the clean bullets and fires.

**SCOPE POV**

One figure on the roof is hit. The other man crawls back and out of sight.

**RIDGE**

> JAMES
> Nice. You got him. Second one is out
> of range.

**SCOPE POV**

Scanning... Another FIGURE, lying on the desert floor.

**RIDGE**

> JAMES
> Twenty meters to the right of the
> building. You got a target.

> SANBORN
> I got him.

> JAMES
> Fire when ready.

**SCOPE POV**

Sanborn's bullet strikes the ground a dozen feet in front of the
man, kicking up a harmless puff of dust.

The man gets up and runs towards the building while firing his
AK-47 back at Sanborn and James. His carbine's muzzle flash,
ineffective at this great range, sparkles in the bright day.

**RIDGE**

> JAMES
> He's moving to the building. Follow
> him. You got him?

> SANBORN
> Got him.

Sanborn pulls the trigger.

**SCOPE POV**

Sanborn's bullet strikes the fleeing man in the upper chest,
blood spurting as the large round throws him dead to the ground.

**RIDGE**

                    JAMES
        You got him. He's down. Good night.
        Thanks for playing.

**SCOPE POV**

The sniper in the building appears in the window.

**BUILDING**

The insurgent sniper team leans out the window and fires at
James and Sanborn.

**RIDGE**

The bullet snaps near James and Sanborn.

                    JAMES
        Window! Window!

                    SANBORN
        Got it.

Sanborn fires.

**SCOPE POV**

Miss! Sanborn's bullet strikes the building just below the
window and the insurgent team withdraws inside.

                    JAMES
        He's still there.

The insurgent, having run to the other side of the building, now
appears in the other window, the left window. James sees his
barrel.

                    JAMES
        Left window! Left window! Got him?

                    SANBORN
        Got him.

Sanborn turns his head away from the gun and makes an audible
exhale to release tension: the sniper breath control technique.
Then he fires a hit; the insurgent slumps in the window.

> JAMES
> He's down.


**SCOPE POV**

The roof of the tall building in the distance bobs in and out of view; the scope dances at this range.

James scans the area. Silence.


**DESERT WIDE**

We mark the passage of time with dust devils spinning across a horizon of lengthening shadows.


**EXT/INT  DEEP RAVINE  HOURS LATER**

The sun lower in the sky. Around the pit, the fallen TEAM LEADER has been pushed to one side, and the living are hanging on to their sanity.

Eldridge and the remaining contractors have exhausted their water supply.

Eldridge is in a sentry position facing east, in the direction of the railroad tracks. The other two contractors are in sentry positions facing south and north.

Sanborn and James are in EXACTLY the same position as when we left them, exposed to the elements. Desert heat and sand have taken their toll on Sanborn especially.


**EXT  SANBORN POV**

The scope BLURS as Sanborn's vision fails for a moment.


**RIDGE**

James notices Sanborn's fatigue.

> JAMES
> Eldridge, grab me the juice out of an
> MRE.

Eldridge digs around the dead TEAM LEADER'S backpack and retrieves a packet of juice, which he passes to James.

James inserts the straw into the juice pack.

He hesitates, not sure if Sanborn will accept the gesture after
all the hostility that's passed between them...

James brings the straw to Sanborn's lips.

At first, Sanborn keeps his attention on the rifle scope.

> JAMES
> Drink.

With some discomfort, Sanborn opens his sun-scorched lips and
sips.

**RAVINE**

Eldridge scans the horizon--

--a small HERD of GOATS amble along the railroad tracks.

He rubs his eyes, looks again--

--*Somewhere within the herd a flutter of fabric*--

Eldridge stiffens.

> ELDRIDGE
> Uh, Will.

> JAMES
> Yeah.

> ELDRIDGE
> At your six o'clock. Movement on the
> tracks.

> JAMES
> Deal with it.

> ELDRIDGE
> Uh, okay.

Eldridge looks down his scope, unsure. James keeps his focus
forward on the building.

> ELDRIDGE
> Should I fire?

> JAMES
> Your call.

Eldridge shifts his weight onto his rifle.

Another flutter of movement at the edge of the tracks.

Eldridge pulls the trigger. Then he pulls it again. And again, emptying his magazine at the distant target.

The goats scatter, revealing a lifeless BODY draped across the tracks.

Eldridge slumps, let's go of his rifle.

                                        TIME CUT TO:


**RAVINE SEVERAL HOURS LATER**

Dusk. Shadows fall over James and Sanborn, both of whom remain lying in the exact same sniping position, although now they are covered head to toe in sand.

There's no movement in the house. No movement on the far ridge. No sign of life anywhere beyond their encampment.

It's just them and the sky and the desert.

                    JAMES
          I think we're done.

                                        CUT TO:


**INT  CAMP VICTORY  JAMES' TRAILER  NIGHT**

Play time: James and Sanborn square off, drunk, swaying, red-faced, fists clenched. When Sanborn nods, James punches him in the stomach.

James smiles; he looks good. The unleashed aggression is like a vitamin to him.

                    JAMES
          That's what you get for hitting your
          team-leader, motherfucker.

With difficulty, Sanborn straightens up and stumbles out of the trailer.

                    SANBORN
          Be right back. I gotta piss.

James lurches towards Eldridge.

                    JAMES
          Owen, another round. That's an order.

                         ELDRIDGE
                    (imitating a young
                    recruit)
          Yes, Sir, Sergeant James Sir.
          You're not very good with people are
          you -- but you're a natural  warrior.

                         JAMES
          You acquitted yourself well on the
          field of battle today, Specialist.

They clink cups. Eldridge gulps his whiskey.

James collapses in his chair.

Eldridge sits down carefully.

                         ELDRIDGE
          I was scared.

                         JAMES
          Everyone is a coward about something.
                    (beat)
          You did good.

As Sanborn loudly stumbles back into the room, he notices by the
door something a little odd under James' bed: a box. It's odd
because there is nothing else in the barren room besides Army-
issue furniture, lights, and the whiskey they've been drinking.

Curious, Sanborn retrieves the box out and sets it on a
makeshift coffee table to get a better look.

                         SANBORN
          Just what do we have here? Will has
          possessions! I didn't know you owned
          anything, Will.

                         ELDRIDGE
          Let's see what you got.

Sanborn pulls out a weathered snapshot of a baby boy.

                         SANBORN
          What's that?

                         JAMES
          That's my son. He's a real tough
          little bastard. Nothing like me.

                         SANBORN
          You're married?

                    JAMES
Well, I had a girlfriend. She got
pregnant and we got married and  then
we divorced. Or, I thought we
divorced. She's still in the house and
she says we're still together. So I
don't know. What does that make her?

                    SANBORN
Dumb - for still being with your ass.

                    JAMES
          (hotly)
She ain't dumb. She's just loyal,
that's all. (beat) What about you guys
- what have you got?

                    SANBORN
My problem is the girl I like I can't
stop from talking about babies.

                    JAMES
Give her your sperm, stud. Make
babies!

                    SANBORN
Nah.

                    JAMES
Go on, you chickenshit. Do it!

                    SANBORN
No, I know when I'm ready and I'm not
ready for that yet.
          (looking around the box,
           finds a circuit board)
And what do we have here?

                    JAMES
          (embarrassed)
Components. Bomb parts. Signatures.

                    SANBORN
I see that. But what are they doing
under your bed?

James pulls out a circuit and gazes reverently at the mechanical
design.

                    JAMES
This one is from the UN building,
flaming car. Dead man switch - boom!
This guy was good. I like him.
          (MORE)

                              JAMES (cont'd)
                    This one was from our first call
                    together. This box is full of stuff
                    that almost killed me.

Eldridge rummages through the box and finds a gold ring hanging
from a cheap chain.

He dangles the ring in front of James.

                              ELDRIDGE
                    What's this one from, Will?

                              JAMES
                    That's my wedding ring. Like I said,
                    stuff that almost killed me.
                         (beat)
                    I think it's interesting to hold
                    something in your hands that could
                    have killed any one of us.

                              SANBORN
                         (looking at the circuit
                          board)
                    It's a piece of junk from Radio Shack.

Eldridge, ever unsure, allies with James.

                              ELDRIDGE
                    It's interesting.

            JAMES                          SANBORN
    I agree. I think it's         I think that punch was harder
    interesting, too.             than I hit you. Therefore, I
                                  owe you a punch. So get up
                                  motherfucker.

James leaps up, pleased to end the conversation.

Sanborn follows, clapping his hands -- cruising for a bruising.

                              ELDRIDGE
                    Hold on, we need some rules. No face
                    shots.

                              SANBORN
                         (laughing)
                    There's gonna be a face shot.

Eldridge picks up a magic marker and tells James to take off his
shirt.

Then he draws a bulls-eye on James' bared stomach.

And as he does, he notices knotty scar tissue.

                         ELDRIDGE
                    What happened?

                         JAMES
                    My mother dropped me at birth.

                         ELDRIDGE                    SANBORN
          Looks like frag scars.          Let it go, Eldridge.

James smiles, raises his arms, exposing his midsection to
Sanborn.

Sanborn winds up for a powerful blow. He leans back, then
launches a gut punch that knocks James to the floor.

James lies there in a heap, laughing.

When he gets up, he's laughing so hard that gleeful tears run
down his face.

                         SANBORN
                    You like that?

                         JAMES
                    That all you got?

Now Sanborn raises his arms, bracing for the blow.

James feints a right cross, fakes a jab, then grabs Sanborn by
the neck and unleashes a brutal uppercut to the solar plexus.
Sanborn collapses, moaning in pain.

                         JAMES
                         (laughing)
                    That's got to hurt.

                         ELDRIDGE
                    You alright?

                         SANBORN
                    Yeah.

                         JAMES
                    Get up, bitch.

James extends his hand to help Sanborn off the floor.

But when Sanborn reaches for help, James rushes him wildly, like
a football tackle, knocking him back to the floor, and, in a
sudden fit of aggression, he then jumps on Sanborn's chest, pins
his arms with his knees and clasps his throat.

                         JAMES
              What have you got now?

                         SANBORN
              Get off me!

                         JAMES
              Come on, what have you got.

                         SANBORN
              Get off of me you freak!!

Sanborn tries to buck James off but he can't dislodge the former
Ranger.

Sanborn redoubles his efforts, throwing his weight this way and
that. Still, James remains on top -- his face twisted with a
macho snarl.

                         JAMES
              We got a wild one here!!

Sanborn bucks harder. But instead of knocking James loose, his
kicking and struggling to get free spurs James to even deeper
levels of male weirdness. And as Sanborn kicks and bucks
underneath him, James pumps his hand like a cowboy at a rodeo,
crying out:

                         JAMES
                 I'm riding him! That's right!! He's a
                 wild one and I'm riding him!! COME ON
                 BITCH!!!

Now Sanborn reaches for his boot knife.

*ECU: knife blade snapping open*

Sanborn jams the blade against James' throat and their eyes
lock.

James smiles like a child. He pats Sanborn's head and laughs.

                         JAMES
                 I'm just kidding motherfucker!!
                 Shit!!!

At last, Sanborn is released. James pats him on the chest.

                    JAMES
You're alright, Sanborn.
         (to Eldridge)
Owen, get this guy another drink.

                                  CUT TO:


**EXT CAMP VICTORY   HOURS LATER**

Sanborn, too drunk to stand, is being guided across the barracks
square by Eldridge and James. When they come to Eldridge's
trailer, James shoulders Sanborn by himself and Eldridge goes
inside.

                  ELDRIDGE
Later.

It's not easy for James to carry Sanborn alone and Sanborn
nearly slips to the ground.

                    JAMES
You need to go on a diet.

They walk a little farther to Sanborn's trailer, passing a
SOLDIER who looks at them curiously. Drinking is not allowed on
US bases in Iraq. James brushes aside the officious look, saying
"he hurt his knee" and guides Sanborn up a set of stairs into
Sanborn's trailer.


**INT. SANBORN'S TRAILER**

James eases Sanborn onto a cot and heads for the door.

                    JAMES
Get some rest.

Sanborn mumbles drunkenly:

                  SANBORN
Hey James, do you think I have what it
takes to put on the suit?

                  JAMES
(beat)
Hell no.
(Beat)
Good night, boy.

**INT  JAMES' TRAILER  LATER THAT NIGHT**

James stumbles inside, flops on the bed, and takes another swig of whiskey.

He lies there and stares at his bomb helmet, which is sitting on a desk adjacent to his cot.

He looks at the helmet... and reaches for it.

Then he brings the helmet over his head and adjusts the straps and unlocks the glass protective masks, so that it snaps down over his face and his entire head is sheathed in the protective metal.

A man encased in his armor.

He leans back in the bed and we HEAR the rasp of James BREATHING...daydreaming...as he re-experiences the feeling of a bomb in his hands, the morbid thrill.

                                        CUT TO:


**EXT/INT HUMVEE  CAMP VICTORY  PARKING LOT**

A massive sandstorm is underway. Howling winds disperse red sand over the entire base, giving it an otherworldly, almost Martian aspect. Throngs of men and their vehicles fight the brutal weather.

**TITLE:**

**Days Left in Bravo Company's Rotation: 16**

Lt. Col. Cambridge comes out of the gloom, approaches the vehicles window, and knocks.

                    CAMBRIDGE
          Mind if I ride along? I'm sick of
          sitting behind a desk all the time.

James shoots Eldridge a look.  Eldridge shrugs.

                    JAMES
          It's a privilege.
               (as Cambridge gets in) )
               (MORE)

                    JAMES (cont'd)
          I don't mean to insult your
          intelligence, Sir, but if the shit
          hits the fan please don't fire out the
          Humvee, the rounds will just bounce
          around and someone might get shot. I
          don't like getting shot.

                    CAMBRIDGE
          Understood, Sergeant.


**EXT. ABU GHRAIB CENTER  BOMBED OUT BUILDING  DAY**

A partially destroyed building fills the screen. A mess of
bricks and rebar. Wind swirls sand up into the air.

**TITLE:**

**DAYS LEFT IN BRAVO COMPANY'S ROTATION: 16**

Nearby, an OLD IRAQI MAN with a DONKEY drawn cart is unloading
new bricks to repair the building.

Farther up the road, a good distance from the building, are two
parked Humvees. Nearby, James and his team are talking to a
small cluster of SOLDIERS.

Eldridge gives Cambridge the drill:

                    ELDRIDGE
          This is a pretty standard mission.
          We're just here to pick up some
          ordnance. Sergeant James is going to
          go see what the deal is. Hopefully,
          we're gone in a couple of minutes

                    JAMES
          Guys, we got to gear up.

                    SANBORN
          For what?

                    JAMES
          Security hasn't gone in. Let's just go
          in quiet, radios off.

                    ELDRIDGE
          Glad you came.

                    CAMBRIDGE
          Stay safe.

## INT BOMBED OUT BUILDING

James, Sanborn and Eldridge enter a landing. The floor is very wet. They cross it, and come to a room that has been severely damaged by a bomb, with rubble everywhere and exposed electrical wires dangling from the ceiling, and busted pipes gushing water. A tea pot sits on a STOVE, steaming hot, and a plate on the table has bread on it.

## WATER LOGGED ROOM

They gingerly investigate a large cavernous room with leaky pipes dripping water onto an oil-slicked floor. We HEAR their breathing, the water DROPLETS falling. Moving tactically, covering all sides of their approach, they press deeper into the building down

## CORRIDOR

A dark corridor which the insurgents have strewn with glass as an early-warning system. Advancing slowly, glass CRUNCHING underfoot, they pass through this corridor into

## CLASSROOM

A classroom lined with student's desks and chairs, beyond which lies another room. James and Sanborn spin quietly into this room, rifles raised, while Eldridge hangs back to cover the corridor.

## INSURGENT LIVING SPACE

They find themselves in a recently used living area. A teapot cooking on a bunsen burner hisses steam. Mattresses and bedding line the walls of the room. The walls are decorated with Jihadist slogans, and a video camera for making recruiting videos has pride of place on a tripod in the center of the room.

Sanborn checks under the mattresses for hidden explosives, finds none, and exchanges a worried look with James.

Moving as one unit they spin into the next room.

## EMPTY ROOM

It's empty, another forboding large space strewn with rubble and garbage. They pass through this area and push open a door to --

**BOMB FACTORY**

Santa's bomb making factory.

In contrast to the spare spaces they've just passed through, this room is overflowing with the tools of a an insurgency that uses bombs as its primary weapon: electronics and explosives of all kinds are everywhere: artillery shells, boxes of batteries, plastic explosives, military manuals, rockets, grenades, stacks of dynamite, tools, magnifying glasses, and soldering guns.

Though a few of these munitions bear the stamps of foreign militaries, most bear insignias in English. It is, ironically, a cache of armaments that formerly belonged to the American military.

The men weave through the piles of explosives, slowly checking every space where a human could possibly be hiding.

At last they're satisfied:

> SANBORN
> Clear!

Eldridge draws near to one desk where a cigarette burns in an ashtray.

> ELDRIDGE
> This cigarette is still smoking!

> SANBORN
> This is all our shit. Motherfucking
> gold mine. Watch out for trips.

**BACK OF ROOM**

In the back half of the room, a plastic curtain hangs over a work table, forming a make-shift sterile room.

Smelling the copper odor of blood and death emanating from behind that curtain, James pushes the plastic to one side.

He draws near to a table, where he sees the DEAD BODY of a YOUNG BOY wearing pants but no shirt. Flies buzz over his bloody bare chest.

> JAMES
> I got something.

Sanborn and Eldridge come beside him, and approach the body cautiously.

The dead young man's chest has been cut open. An artillery shell is shoved inside the cavity where the heart used to beat. Wires protrude from the shell.

James shakes his head no as Sanborn moves closer to the body and inspects the wiring in the chest.

The boy's FACE, half in shadow, is so disfigured by bruises that it's hard to identify. But it might be someone familiar to James.

>                    JAMES
>          I know this kid. His name is Beckham.
>          He sells DVDs.

Sanborn ignores that and turns to Eldridge.

>                    SANBORN
>          You ever see a body bomb before?

Eldridge shakes his head, pulling his neck scarf up over his nose.

>                    SANBORN
>          This is disgusting, let's get out of
>          here.

>                    JAMES
>          Eldridge, grab all the C4 and det cord
>          you can get your hands on. Let's get
>          the rest of it out of here and just
>          blow it in place.

>                    SANBORN
>          Roger that.

Sanborn and Eldridge leave James alone with the body.

He stares at the boy.


**EXT BOMBED OUT BUILDING**

Cambridge, with limited Iraqi language skills, is trying to speak to a MAN piling rocks in the back of his donkey cart.

>                    CAMBRIDGE
>          What are you doing? Moving the rocks?

The Iraqi peasant replies in Arabic, motioning to the rocks and his cart.

> CAMBRIDGE
> That's very nice. It's a little unsafe
> today. So maybe - I don't know - I'm
> thinking maybe we should move.

**INT BODY BOMB**

James steps away.

**EXT BOMBED OUT BUILDING**

Sanborn and Eldridge meet up outside.

> SANBORN
> You okay?

> EDLDRIDGE
> Yeah. You?

**INT   BOMBED OUT BUILDING   MOMENTS LATER**

James turns away from the body.  Thinks.

Eldridge arrives with the C4.  The look on James' face concerns
him.

> ELDRIDGE
> You alright man?

> JAMES
> Yeah, no one in or out.

Eldridge nods.  Makes a hasty exit.

James pulls C4 blocks from his pack and arranges them around the
body. He plugs a blasting cap into the C4. In doing so he finds
himself drawn to the dead boy's eyes, which seem *somehow* to
stare directly at him.

James tries to keep his feelings in check and his mind on the
task by arranging the charges and preparing the detonation.

But he can't. *The war has finally reached him.*

> JAMES
> (into walkie)
> Cancel the det.

In one fluid motion James removes the charges and takes off his
helmet.

He closes the boy's eyes.

And slams his fists on the table.

                                                        CUT TO:


**EXT. BUILDING**

Sanborn and Eldridge grab water by the Humvee.

                    SANBORN
          What the fuck is he doing?

                    ELDRIDGE
          I don't know.


**CAMBRIDGE AT THE DONKEY CART**

Now there are a few IRAQI MEN gathered near the donkey cart.
Cambridge is doing his best to communicate.

                    CAMBRIDGE
          Hello, how are you?

                    IRAQI MAN
          Where are you from?

                    CAMBRIDGE
          New York. The Big Apple.

                    IRAQI MAN
          I'm from Iraq.

                    CAMBRIDGE
          I love it here. This is a beautiful
          place. But today, it's not too safe
          here, so I think we need to move.
          Please.


**INT BOMBED OUT BUILDING**

James carefully checks the boy's body for trip wires, then
proceeds the snip the wires which were sown into the boy's
stomach.

One by one, he cuts them.

He inserts his hands into the boy's abdomen and removes the
artillery shell bomb that had been diabolically placed there.

He wipes his face, smearing blood, then covers the body in a
white cloth.

> JAMES
> (into walkie)
> I'm coming down.

The boy's blood seeps through the cloth and stains it red.

**INT  BOMBED OUT BUILDING  STAIRS**

James carries the boy's body down the narrow corridor. The head
and feet bump the sides.

**EXT  STREET/BOMBED OUT BUILDING**

James brings the body out carries it to a blue and white pickup
TRUCK emblazoned with the logo of the Iraqi National Police
pulls up to their position.

A pair of POLICEMEN get out and after a few words with James,
they load the body.

**EXT  BOMBED OUT BUILDING**

James watches the police truck drive away. He then moves for the
Humvee, motioning for Cambridge to load up.

**INT  HUMVEE**

Sanborn and Eldridge sit across from each other, watching James.

> ELDRIDGE
> ...So you think it was that little
> base rat?

> SANBORN
> No I don't.

> ELDRIDGE
> You positive?

> SANBORN
> Sure. I don't know. They all look the
> same, right?

> ELDRIDGE
> I don't know. Will seemed sure. But
> that was weird.

                        SANBORN
          Very weird.


**CAMBRIDGE AT THE DONKEY CART**

Cambridge, losing patience with what is now a small crowd of
Iraqis, motions with his M4.

                        CAMBRIDGE
          Please, just move. Please. Ishmee
          (pronouncing the Arabic incorrectly).

The crowd slowly disperses, amid grumbling and cursing.
Cambridge waves patronizingly at them as they go, saying "thank
you, bye-bye," etc.  He doesn't notice that one of the older men
has left on the ground <u>a white rice bag</u>.


**INT HUMVEE**

Simultaneously, the conversation in the Humvee continues:

                        ELDRIDGE
          But then Will's pretty weird. He keeps
          bomb parts under his bed.

                        SANBORN
          I bet you he doesn't keep any of these
          parts under his bed.

James cracks the door of the Humvee, leans inside, sees
Cambridge -

                        JAMES
                (shouting to Cambridge)
          Let's go!

**Through the HUMVEE windshield:** Cambridge, now pleased that the
crowd has gone, waves good-bye to the entire neighborhood, and,
hearing James, steps towards the Humvee, passing <u>the white rice
bag,</u> which suddenly --

--*explodes in a A SICKENING **BLAST***

--*obliterating Cambridge*

--*sending his head crashing into the HUMVEE, along with a cloud
of debris which instantly blackens the windshield and blots out
the sun and our view of everything -*

**INT/EXT HUMVEE**

CRIES of "IED!" "IED" as our three soldiers stumble out of the vehicle into the rancid air, while other soldiers, dashing to the scene from all sides, scramble to restore order and shout "it's the commander" "watch your six", etc.

We follow Eldridge, stunned, as he walks into the aftermath and finds a smoking helmet on the ground.

He picks it up.

Its nylon cover is burning; the inside is charred.

Eldridge looks down and sees body parts and bits of uniform strewn on the ground.

> ELDRIDGE
> Where's Cambridge? Cambridge! Come on, we got to go! (beat) Doc?

James rushes to Eldridge's side.

> JAMES
> He's dead.

> ELDRIDGE
> *I just saw him! He was walking right here!*

James pulls Eldridge into a bear hug. Eldridge sobs.

> JAMES
> He's dead. He's dead.
> (beat)
> But you're alright, buddy. You're alright.

CUT TO:

**EXT CAMP VICTORY DUSK**

As the sun sets behind him, James leans against a power pole and dials a SATELLITE PHONE.

He hangs up.

Dials again.

**INT SUBURBAN HOME - HALFWAY AROUND THE WORLD**

In a modest mid-Western kitchen, the phone rings. A young WOMAN holding a BABY rushes to get it.

> WOMAN
> Hello?
> (beat)
> Will? Hello?

Silence on the other end of the line.

**EXT CAMP VICTORY DUSK**

James hangs up and shoves the phone back in his pocket.

**EXT  CAMP VICTORY  MESS TENT  MORNING**

James, smoking, twitchy, watching something... the OLDER IRAQI MAN who sells DVDs at Beckham's usual table. Although Beckham is not there, the man organizes his DVDs, business as usual. James stalks up to him.

> JAMES
> Hey, let me ask you a question, what
> happened to the little kid that used
> to work here?

The man shakes his head.

> DVD MAN
> Sorry man, no English.

> JAMES
> No English? Now you don't speak
> English. The little kid? Beckham is
> his name. He sells DVDs.

> DVD MAN
> DVD? One DVD five dollars.

James turns to a nearby INFANTRY GUARD.

> JAMES
> Excuse me, soldier, are you in charge
> of this area?

> GUARD
> What's up?

# STILLS

Jeremy Renner playing the mercurial team leader, Sergeant James, a man who has fallen for war's addictive allure.

Anthony Mackie as the forceful, quick-witted Sergeant Sanborn,
trying to make it home alive.

Brian Geraghty playing Specialist Eldridge, a bundle of nerves and bravado.

Guy Pearce as the easy-going veteran, Sergeant Thompson.

Ralph Fiennes, British mercenary.

David Morse, playing Colonel Reed.

Shooting *The Hurt Locker* in Jordan.

Jeremy Renner as Sergeant James, awed by the destruction of an IED.

(from left to right) Director of Photography Barry Ackroyd, Writer Mark
Boal, and Director Kathryn Bigelow on location in Jordan.

Writer Mark Boal, in Baghdad, Iraq, 2004.

                         JAMES
          That guy over there could be an
          insurgent. (referring to the DVD
          merchant) How do we know he's not
          giving intel to his buddies, telling
          them where to drop mortars?

                         GUARD
          I think he's just selling DVDs.

                         JAMES
          He's a security risk. You should get
          rid of him.

                         GUARD
          He's just selling DVDs. All the
          merchants are cleared. I couldn't do
          anything to him without the say-so
          from my C.O.

James, agitated, seeing that he has no hope of prevailing, turns
away and trudges back into Camp Victory's maze.

                                        CUT TO:


**EXT. CAMP VICTORY MESS TENT   HOURS LATER**

It's the end of the day and the DVD seller packs up his wares to
close shop. James, in sunglasses, sweatshirt covering his army
fatigues, watches him do this, and then follows the man to his
truck. As the man starts the engine, James jumps in the
passenger side and threatens with his pistol.

                         JAMES
          Does this change anything? Speak
          English now, don't you?
          Drive!


**INT IRAQI TRUCK**

The truck passes through a middle-class Baghdad neighborhood and
comes to a stop at a house surrounded by an 8-foot high concrete
wall.

159                      JAMES                          159
          This is the house? Beckham's house?

The driver nods, sort of.

                         JAMES
          Wait here.

**EXT BAGHDAD STREET   NIGHT**

James gets out and jogs to the house. He tries the front gate, sees that it is locked, and while he does the car drives off.

If he cares, he doesn't show it. James scales the wall and drops inside the front courtyard.

**EXT IRAQI HOUSE   COURTYARD**

A modest courtyard. Light comes from one window in the house, the rest is dark. Crickets. Inside, a TV is playing. James tries the front door. It opens.

**INT IRAQI HOUSE   HALLWAY**

In a dark hallway. Murmuring of a television. James moves towards the noise.

**INT IRAQI HOUSE   ANTECHAMBER**

James comes to an antechamber. Behind it is <u>a very low stone archway</u>. He goes through the archway, where -

**INT IRAQI HOUSE   LIVING ROOM**

A MAN -- call him KALIM -- older, fifties, dressed in Western fashion, is busy at the sink, washing dishes. James walks in, gun raised. Kalim drops a dish. James puts his fingers to his lips, shhhh.

                    JAMES
          Do you speak English?

                    KALIM
          English, French, Arabic.

                    JAMES
              (quietly)
          Good. Open your vest. Stay there. Tell
          me what you know about Beckham.

                    KALIM
          For whom?

                    JAMES
          Beckham. The 12-year old boy, the body
          bomb.

                    KALIM
          Beckham? I don't know. But please sit
          down. I am professor Kalim, this is my
          home. You are a guest. Please sit
          down.

                    JAMES
          I'm a guest...I'm just looking for the
          people responsible.

                    KALIM
          You are CIA, no? I am very pleased to
          have CIA in my home. Please, sit.

As his certainty slips away, James hears rustling and spins to
see

-- a WOMAN, older, matronly, carrying a tea tray.  She sees
James, his gun, and starts cursing him in Arab, appalled that an
armed American would come to her house.

James steps back. Her cursing grows fiercer. She raises her tea
tray.

                    KALIM
          Be careful! The gun can go off.

Undaunted, she throws the tray at James. He twists to avoid it,
takes a few steps to the door, and ends up HITTING his HEAD
badly on the concrete archway as he runs out of the house.


**EXT. IRAQI HOUSE/STREET**

James is shaken. He looks around and down the street. *He
runs...and runs*...Blood runs from the wound on his head as he
navigates the busy Iraqi neighborhood at night, running down
streets teeming with SHOPPERS who stare at him ominously,
dodging traffic, moving past OLD MEN smoking at a CAFE who note
his panic, by a BUTCHER SHOP where an entire COW CARCASS is
being unloaded, and on and on... we stay with his eyes.

Off the a screeching car as James dashes across a street, we

                                             CUT TO:


**EXT  CAMP VICTORY GATE  NIGHT**

James, hands held high over his head, walks up to one of the
camp's check-points, shouting:

                    JAMES
            USA Friendly coming in!

Powerful flood lights switch on, blinding him. Then the
screaming of hyped up guards:

          GUARDS                         GUARDS
Stop, get the fuck down. On    Don't fucking move!
your knees!

          GUARDS                         GUARDS
Stop!                          On your knees, on your knees!!

James sinks to his knees.

          GUARD                          GUARD
Open your fucking jacket!      Cover!!

James unzips his sweatshirt and declares:

                    JAMES
            I have a weapon!

A guard armed with a shotgun charges out of the glare and kicks
James to the ground, pinning his knee into his back.

                    GUARD
            Searching!

The guard finds James' pistol. He shouts:

          GUARD                          JAMES
Gun!! Weapon's clear!!         Like I said. (beat) Do you
                               want to look at my I.D.?

                    GUARD
            What are you doing out here?

                    JAMES
                (gasping)
            I was at a whore house.

                    GUARD
            (thinking it over)
            Okay, if I let you in, will you tell
            me where it is exactly?

                                        CUT TO:

**EXT   CAMP VICTORY   NIGHT**

James steps into his trailer. His walkie, sitting on a desk, CRACKLES to life.

> SANBORN
> (over walkie)
> I repeat, do you copy? Do you have your ears on? James?

> JAMES
> (into walkie)
> Yeah, this is James. What's up?

**INT   HUMVEE   MINUTES LATER**

In a bustling parking lot, aglow with headlights from Humvees and troop carries, we find James running towards one Humvee, which he jumps into. Sanborn is at the wheel and not amused.

> SANBORN
> We have a tanker explosion in the Green Zone. We have to do a post-blast assessment, see if it was a suicide bomber and if so how he pulled it off.
> (beat)
> So where did you say you were again?

> JAMES
> I didn't, Sergeant. Let's go.

> SANBORN
> What happened to your head, James?

James gives no reply. He turns to Eldridge.

> JAMES
> Ready? Game face buddy.

As the Humvee rolls out of the base,

> SANBORN PRELAP
> USA Friendlies coming in!

CUT TO:

**EXT   BAGHDAD STREET   LATE NIGHT**

A helicopter spotlight illuminates a Hieronymus Bosch nightmare of tangled limbs and body parts.

Then fires, smoke, and the cries of wailing grievers and wounded carried on stretchers, ambulances, police, fire trucks...the ghastly, frantic aftermath of a major detonation.

Their combat flashlights send piercing white beams into this grim spectacle, while in the distance a huge fire, a GLOWING RED INFERNO at the end of the block, lights what we now see is a blast radius that extends for a nearly a mile.

Moving towards the glowing fire, past ten foot high flames and the remains of houses pulverized to concrete and glass, rubble piles, past screaming women and more bloody wounded being carried away by IRAQI POLICE... they pause to try and help Iraqi police save a man pinned under a car. He's dragged away like a rag doll.

They press on towards the inferno and stop when they notice a hunk of metal.

>                         JAMES
>             Oil tanker?

>                         SANBORN
>             Yup. Pretty long flight.

Moving ahead, the men split up, navigating different paths through this hectic apocalypse:


**ELDRIDGE**

A Bhurka-clad WOMAN appears out of the distant flames and haze, looking disoriented, in apparent shock. Behind her is a blazing car.

On the ground beside the car lies a single black loafer.

Eldridge sees the lone shoe and is at a loss to process its significance.

Another mind-numbing, soul-numbing casualty of war.


**SANBORN**

At a gigantic rubble pile, Sanborn reaches down to remove chunks of stone covering a BODY.

The stone slides away but another falls in its place.

Sanborn looks down, sees a second man, or what's left of a man: head and torso but no legs -- just stumps, twitching.

Around him, GRIEVING FAMILIES pick through the dead and dying with IRAQI MEDICS.

## JAMES

Drawing near to the inferno, he moves past burning palm trees which erupt into a fountain of embers.

And comes at last to the burning steel carcase of...

## OIL TANKER

an OIL TANKER.

From what's left of the twisted metal sub-frame flames twenty feet high scorch the night, like the maw of hell on earth.

James stares, transfixed by the burning...the imprint of some insurgent's plan.

His face hardens now in a way we haven't seen before, and as the fire flickers on his features he seems lost in a private war of his own.

The insurgents are out there *somewhere*.

Ahab and the Whale.

## SANBORN AND ELDRIDGE

Sanborn and Eldridge look helplessly at a girl who is trapped on the landing of a half-destroyed building. She cries for her father.

Behind them, several platoons of U.S. SOLDIERS and IRAQI POLICE arrive to secure the boundaries of the blast zone.

                                                              CUT TO:

## EDGE OF BLAST RADIUS

James approaches a LEMON GROVE which lies just beyond the fire's reach.

As Sanborn and Eldridge walk up behind him, James touches a UNBLEMISHED LEMON nestled among the thorns.

                              JAMES
                    This is the edge of the blast radius.

Sanborn comes into view. James nods to him, then stares into the distance, a man possessed.

                    JAMES
          So where's our trigger man?

                    SANBORN
          Burnt up in the flames. Suicide
          bomber. You'll never find a body.

                    JAMES
          But what if there was no body. What if
          it was a remote det?
                    (beat)
          A really good bad guy hides out in the
          dark, right? This is a perfect vantage
          point outside the blast radius to set
          back and watch us --

                    ELDRIDGE
          You want to go out there?

                    JAMES
          Yes I do.

                    ELDRIDGE
          I could stand to get in some trouble.

Sanborn looks at James and looks at the bandage on his head.

                    SANBORN
          No, man, this is bullshit.
          You got --what?-- *three* infantry
          platoons here whose job it is to go
          haji hunting. That's not our job.

                    JAMES
          You don't say 'No' to me, Sergeant. I
          say 'No' to you. You know there are
          guys watching us right now.
                    (on the move)
          We're going.

James glowers at Sanborn and Eldridge and moves deeper into an unlit field behind the lemon grove.

Eldridge shoots Sanborn a sympathetic glance and follows James.

Sanborn watches them recede into the darkness. Then he runs after his team.

**EXT  FIELD**

They move across the dark field, three abreast into the enveloping night.

We gradually lose sight of them in BLACKNESS. Seeing nothing, we HEAR, however, their BREATHING, and gravel CRUNCHING underfoot.

After a long moment of no visibility...they're faintly visible again in dim florescent light and we see:

**EXT  PARKING LOT**

A shadowy parking lot filled with marooned cars, beyond which lies a neighborhood of one-story homes and narrow alleys.

Amid the cars, the men come across the bullet-shaped hull of an intact oil tanker. They crouch beside it, whispering:

> JAMES
> We know where the oil tanker came from.

> SANBORN
> It's the same kind.

> JAMES
> We're close. These alleys are probably set up in a grid. We're going to split up to flush them out. Sanborn take the first alley. Eldridge take two. I got three. Rally point at your intersection. Ready? Move!

> SANBORN
> Wait? Rally point? When?

But James has already dashed into the third alley.

**ALLEY  TWO**

Eldridge, walking slowly, not sure he likes being alone.

**ALLEY  THREE**

James runs confidently, sees a few kids in a doorway and tells them to scoot.

**ALLEY ONE**

Sanborn runs to make up for being the last to leave.

**ALLEY TWO**

Eldridge peers into an abandoned house. He thinks he hears something.

Spins.

It's nothing.

**ALLEY ONE**

Sanborn slows. Catches his breath when suddenly --

--*BLAM, BLAM, BLAM - the staccato of GUNFIRE slaps off the concrete*--

Sanborn dashes full speed back to the alley's opening.

**ALLEY THREE**

James turns, runs hard back into--

**SANBORN AND JAMES**

--the first intersection, where he sees Sanborn and shouts

                    JAMES
          You got contact?!

                  SANBORN
          Who is it?! What's going on?

                    JAMES
          What have you got?!

                  SANBORN
          It's Eldridge!!

**ALLEY TWO**

They come to Eldridge's alley where they see that a body lies on the ground. They run to it.

> JAMES
> Man down!!

> SANBORN
> Eldridge!!

As they draw close they see not Eldridge but the BODY of an
Iraqi insurgent, dead from gunshot wounds.

> JAMES
> It's not him.

> SANBORN
> He's gone?!

A moment of decision.

> SANBORN
> That way is towards the tanker,
> troops.

They run down the alley into a maze of narrow streets and dimly
lit corridors.


**NARROW STREET**

Turning a corner, they catch a fleeting glimpse of Eldridge
being dragged away by TWO INSURGENTS.

Before they can fire, the men are gone.


**CORNER**

They run to this corner and prepare to spin around it and shoot.

James hands Sanborn his flashlight.

> JAMES
> Hit 'em with both lights. One, two,
> three!


**DARK CORNER**

They spin around the corner and flash light revealing NOTHING
but an empty street.

**NEXT ALLEY**

They sprint to the next block, and again see Eldridge being
dragged.

>                    JAMES
>           One, two, three.

Again, they aim and spin: Sanborn shines the light - beams
Eldridge and the two insurgents -- and James FIRES two short
bursts from his M4.

The two insurgents collapse.

But Eldridge also goes down.

Running up, James and Sanborn see the insurgents are motionless,
shot clean.

One bullet, however, has gone astray into Eldridge's leg and
he's bleeding profusely.

>                    JAMES
>           Eldridge you okay?

>                    ELDRIDGE
>           I'm hit!

As James and Sanborn apply first aide:

>                    SANBORN
>           You hit him in the leg!

>                    ELDRIDGE
>                (panting)
>           Am I dead?

>                    SANBORN
>           No, you're alright.

>                    JAMES
>           You're fine.

Eldridge looks to Sanborn for confirmation that wound is indeed
not mortal.

>                    ELDRIDGE
>           *Am I dead? Am I dead? Am I dead?*

As Sanborn and James yank Eldridge off the ground, he screams in pain.

                                                    CUT TO:


**INT  CAMP VICTORY SHOWER STALLS  LATER THAT NIGHT**

James trudges into an empty bathroom and looks at himself in the mirror. Sees the faraway expression of a man lost to the war.

His shirt is crimson with Eldridge's blood.

He steps inside a shower stall, still dressed in full battle rattle, and turns on the hot faucet.

The water streams over him...and he lets go, punching the wall, thrashing his arms, then sinking down sobbing, broken, as his uniform soaks through and the reddish pink water swirls down the drain.


**EXT  CAMP VICTORY  HEAD SHED  MORNING**

Looking fine and wearing a fresh clean uniform, James strides purposely out of the head shed toward a waiting Humvee in the parking lot.

He sees on the other side of the parking lot... none other than Beckham, who happily shouts to him:

                    BECKHAM
          Hey, what's up man? Hey Boomala,
          Boomala, wanna buys some DVDs, play
          some soccer!

James stops. He stares. What can he say? The boy is fine.

His jihad was pointless. Insane.

Unable to face the kid and unwilling to explain, James turns away and stiffly gets into the Humvee.

The Humvee roars to life and drives away.

Beckham watches it go, hurt, confused.

Prelap: the ROTAR WASH of a helicopter preparing to fly.

**EXT  CAMP VICTORY  TARMAC  MORNING**

Two SOLDIERS load Eldridge, strapped to a stretcher, onto a
transport helicopter.

Sanborn and James run across the helipad to wish him good-bye.

>                    JAMES
>           How you doing? Doc says you'll be
>           okay.

>                    ELDRIDGE
>           My femur is shattered in nine places.
>           He said I'll be walking in six months
>           if, I'm lucky.

>                    JAMES
>           Six ain't bad.

>                    ELDRIDGE
>           Not bad? It fucking sucks man.

Eldridge is jostled as he gets put down; he cries out in pain.

>                    ELDRIDGE
>                (angrily)
>           You see that! That's what happens when
>           you shoot somebody, you motherfucker.

>                    JAMES
>           I'm sorry. Sorry.

>                    ELDRIDGE
>           You're sorry? Fuck you, Will.
>           *Really* *fuck you*. Thanks for saving my
>           life but we didn't have to go out
>           looking for trouble so you could get
>           your adrenaline fix, you fucking war
>           monger.

James is crestfallen.

A U.S. MEDIVAC CREW MEMBER looks at Sanborn and gives a hand
signal to wrap it up: time to go.

>                    ELDRIDGE
>                (to Sanborn)
>           Take care of yourself, Owen.

                    SANBORN
            (grabbing Eldridge's hand)
        Get home safe. See you on the other
        side.

As the helicopter door slams closed, Eldridge shouts "lets get
out of this desert."

James and Sanborn step back from the rotor wash.

James turns to say something to Sanborn. But he's already
walking away.

                    SOLDIER PRELAP
                (shouting)
        Don't move! If you keep walking, we
        will shoot you!

                                            CUT TO:


**EXT BAGHDAD STREET CHECKPOINT   LATE AFTERNOON**

A young SERGEANT at a checkpoint raises his M4 and shouts
nervously at a bewildered Iraqi MAN in a BLACK SUIT. The man's
hands are raised. He's standing alone in the middle of a square
which has been cleared of all other pedestrians, and which is
flanked by US ARMY soldiers and a TRANSLATOR disguising his
identity by wearing a black ski mask.

                    SERGEANT
        Don't move! Keep that translator back!

                    TRANSLATOR
        But the bomb was forced on him.

                    SERGEANT
        Don't move. Stay still. If you keep
        walking we will shoot you.

SHOUTING IN ARABIC as the translator conveys this command.

**TITLE:**

**DAYS LEFT IN BRAVO COMPANY'S ROTATION: 2**

James wearing his bomb suit, approaches the scene, while Sanborn
follows close behind him in the Humvee.

                    SERGEANT
        Keep that translator back.

One of the soldiers grabs the translator, while others, seeing James, shout "give him room," "let him through," etc.

                    TRANSLATOR
               (to the soldier)
          But the bomb was forced on him.
          Against his will. He is not a bad man!

James and the Sergeant huddle.

                    SERGEANT
          He came walking up to our checkpoint,
          said he had a bomb strapped to him. He
          was sorry. He didn't want it to go
          off. Then he started begging us to
          take it off him.

                    TRANSLATOR
               (to James)
          Help this man. He's not a bad man.

                    SANBORN
          Not a bad man? He's got a bomb
          strapped to him.
               (to James)
          This is a trap. He wants to draw us
          close.

                    JAMES
               (to translator)
          Tell him to open his shirt, slowly. I
          need to see what's inside.

The translator SHOUTS in Arabic.

The MAN unbuttons his jacket, revealing...

*Clamped to his chest is a metal cage, locked with padlocks, and loaded with blocks of C4 wrapped in nails.*

                    JAMES
               (to the soldier)
          I'd need a seventy five meter
          perimeter.
               (to translator)
          Tell him to get on his knees and touch
          the sky. Get down!

The translator SHOUTS. The man in the BLACK SUIT, gripped with despair, drops to his knees and raises his hands.

                    SERGEANT
          Can we just shoot him?

As James considers that option when --

                    TRANSLATOR
          *NO. He's not a bad man. He has a*
          *family. The bomb was forced on him. He*
          *is asking for help. Only help.*

                    JAMES
               (to translator)
          I want you to get back. I got it.

Sanborn pulls James aside for a private moment and pleads with
him to be careful:

                    SANBORN
          We've had our differences. Eldridge.
          It happened. That's water under the
          bridge. But this -- this is suicide.

James considers. Sanborn's right, of course. But he can't help
himself. Like a moth to a flame, this is what he does.

                    JAMES
          That's why it's called a suicide bomb,
          right?

Sanborn reluctantly seals James in the helmet.

They bang fists.


**DOWNRANGE NEAR SUICIDE BOMBER**

James grabs a nearby soldier's walkie, then starts the walk
downrange. Soldiers moving back to their perimeter...
PEDESTRIANS gathering for a look.  Soldiers scattering them
quickly.

Black Suit smiles thinly as James nears. James nods at him. The
man nods, frightened.

                    BLACK SUIT
          Inshalla. Inshalla.

                    JAMES
          Put your hands up!

                    TRANSLATOR
          He says he has a family,

James kneels down to get a closer look at the bomb strapped to
the man's belly. He takes out his 9mm and puts it on the guy's
forehead. Cocks the trigger.

> JAMES
> Look, it would be a lot easier for me
> to disarm this if I just shoot you. Do
> you understand?

BLACK SUIT replies in Arabic.

> JAMES
> (into walkie)
> What is he saying?

**UPRANGE FROM SUICIDE BOMBER**

> TRANSLATOR
> (over walkie)
> He says, I don't wish to die. I have a
> family. Please take this off me.

**DOWNRANGE NEAR SUICIDE BOMBER**

James holds his walkie up for the man to hear the translator.

> JAMES
> (headset)
> Tell him to put his hands behind his
> head or I will be very happy to shoot
> him.

Translator conveys this to BLACK SUIT in Arabic. BLACK SUIT
starts yelling in Arabic.  Forehead wet with sweat.

> TRANSLATOR
> (over walkie)
> *He says, please hurry he has a family.*

> JAMES
> (to translator)
> Look, it's not what I said. Tell him
> to put his hands behind his head or I
> will shoot him.

James holds the walkie up to the man's ear, "listen," "do you
understand?"

Now James sinks to his knees and examines the bomb, all the
while keeping his pistol on the man's head.  There is a FOREST
OF WIRES. He pushes them aside, revealing a cheap Casio digital
WATCH, *which is counting down from five minutes.*

> JAMES
> (headset)
> Sanborn, we got a timer. We got a lot
> of wires. I need a little help on
> this.

> SANBORN
> (over headset)
> Roger that, what do you need?

James feels around the bomb. It's strapped to the BLACK SUIT man
with heavy gauge metal. The man shakes.

> JAMES
> (headset)
> Bolt cutters. But you got two minutes
> to get down here.

> SANBORN
> (over walkie)
> Roger that. I'll be there in thirty
> seconds.

**HUMVEE**

Sanborn is already running towards the truck when he hears
James.

**DOWNRANGE NEAR SUICIDE BOMBER**

James presses the man's head to comfort him.

> JAMES
> (to man)
> I know. It's okay. You're alright.

*The Casio watch is at 4:30.*

**UPRANGE FROM SUICIDE BOMBER**

Sanborn runs hard with the bolt cutters.

**DOWNRANGE NEAR SUICIDE BOMBER**

Sanborn hands James the cutters.

The man is crying.

Sanborn sees the Casio. It reads 4:00

> SANBORN
> You weren't kidding.

> JAMES
> Nope.

James works the cutter blade.

**ECU:** Bolt Cutter. It SCRAPES futilely against the metal.

> JAMES
> (sotto)
> What is this made out of?

> SANBORN
> Case hardened steel.

James doubles his effort.

**ECU:** Bolt Cutter. The blade bites the steel, but it doesn't give. James squeezes with all his might.

> SANBORN
> What's our time?

> JAMES
> Two minutes.

> JAMES
> We'd need torch to get this off.

> SANBORN
> We don't have one of those in the
> truck. He's a dead man.

**ECU:** Casio Watch 1:46.

> JAMES
> Hold on let me think. We got this. I
> can handle it. I'm going to look at
> the back.

Sanborn nods. *His hand is starting to shake.*

James goes behind the man, and rips open the back of his shirt, revealing the back of the bomb.

Here too it is a welded band, but the metal looks thinner. James works it with the cutter.

**ECU:** Casio Watch 1:30.

                JAMES
We don't have enough time, Sanborn. We
don't have enough time. I have to get
these bolts off.

                SANBORN
We at a minute and a half, we got to
get out of here.

                JAMES
I'll handle this. Go.

                SANBORN
Look, Will, come on --

                JAMES
Go.

                SANBORN
Fuck him, Come on, man. James --

                JAMES
Sanborn you have forty five seconds.
<u>YOU HAVE FORTY FIVE SECONDS. JUST
LEAVE!</u>

                SANBORN
<u>He's a dead man, Will!</u>

                JAMES
GO!

Sanborn runs uprange.

                SANBORN
            (shouting to soldiers)
    *GET BACK!!! EVERYBODY GET BACK!!!*

The soldiers turn and run.

James strains to clip the metal bar of the lock, putting all of
his weight into the effort. Finally, the blades slices.

**ECU:** broken lock falls to the ground.

James sees that he has four more locks more to cut. The time is
ticking down to 20 seconds.

James brings himself face-to-face with the man he can't save.

                    JAMES
I can't There's too many locks. I
can't do it. I can't get it off. I'm
sorry.

                    BLACK SUIT
*(in Arabic)*
*Please, please, please--*

                    JAMES
I'm sorry. You hear me? I'm sorry?

                    BLACK SUIT
(in Arabic)
*Help me. Help me!*

James drops the bolt cutter, kneels down in front of the man, and shakes his head. That's it.

The man understands James' gesture. He reaches forward, grabbing James' suit.

                    BLACK SUIT
*(in Arabic)*
*No! No! Please*

James brushes his hand away.

                    JAMES
I'm sorry.

James turns his back to the man and runs for cover.

--James running, arms akimbo

--The Black Suit man stands up and cries out to ALLAH!

**BOOM!!**

-- He explodes and *a hailstorm of particulate matter comes flying at 22,000 feet per second straight at us*

-- chunks of molten metal hit James, knocking him to the ground

--Sanborn, diving to keep the translator behind a barrier, is grazed by shrapnel.

**EXT   DOWNRANGE/BLAST SITE**

James' white face; blood seeps from his nose. Then as if overcoming great resistance his heart turns over with a loud beating. And as Sanborn recovers and shouts orders, "everybody out" in the background, James opens his eyes to the sky.

A KITE flutters overhead.

                                                    CUT TO:


**EXT   HUMVEE   DUSK**

The Humvee chugs through a crowded neighborhood. Traffic thickening.  Shadows against a dimming sky.


**INT   HUMVEE   DUSK**

James drives. Sanborn is in the passenger seat covered in grime and dust.

                         JAMES
              You alright?

                         SANBORN
              No man.  I hate this place

James passes Sanborn some Gatorade.

                         JAMES
              Have a hit.

Sanborn drinks, grateful, and puts the Gatorade down. Then he looks at James.

                         SANBORN
              I'm not ready to die, James.

                         JAMES
              You're not going to die out here, bro.

Sanborn shakes his head. Unconsciously, his fingers touch his neck, finding the exposed area above the collar of his body armor.

                         SANBORN
              Another two inches.  Shrapnel goes
              zing -- slices my throat. I bleed out
              like a pig in the sand.
              Nobody will give a shit.
                         (MORE)

110

SANBORN (cont'd)
I mean my parents, they care, but they don't count. Who else?
(beat)
I don't even have a son.

JAMES
You're going to have plenty of time for that.

SANBORN
No man, I'm done.
(beat)
I want a son. I want a little boy, Will.

A long beat.

SANBORN
I mean, how do you do it? Take the risk?

JAMES
I don't know. I guess I don't think about it.

SANBORN
But you know what I'm talking about, right? Every time we go out, you throw the dice. You recognize that, right?

JAMES
Yeah. I do. But I don't know why. Do you know why -- I am the way I am?

Sanborn thinks on this.  After a beat -

SANBORN
No I don't.

They exchange a long look. Brothers at last.

**EXT HUMVEE**

A gang of laughing KIDS throw rocks at the armored Humvee.

TIME CUT TO:

**INT  KNOXVILLE, TENNESSEE  SUPERMARKET  MONTHS LATER**

We're walking with James down a wide, polished aisle, past shelves of frozen treats glistening behind reflective glass, in the shiny and perfectly sterile cathedral to consumerism otherwise known as a supermarket.

James looks different here, awkward, less sure of himself. With his hair grown-in and his dreamy expression, he could be just another suburban softy pushing a shopping cart.

He's home but this is clearly not where he lives.

A beautiful young WOMAN approaches him from the other end of the aisle. She too is pushing a shopping cart and in it is a small BOY. She smiles at James and says:

> YOUNG WOMAN
> Honey, will you grab some cereal and
> I'll meet you at the checkout.

CONNIE JAMES smiles again and pats her husband on the shoulder. As she walks away, he mumbles:

> JAMES
> Where's the cereal?

But she's already out of ear shot.


**CEREAL AISLE**

James stares at the rows and rows of cereal boxes, a medley of different brands all containing the same sugar and coloring and starch.

He looks this way and that.

Thrown by the abundant choices after the starkness of Baghdad, he can't decide which brand is his.

He reaches for a box, then pulls back, still unsure of himself.

Giving up, he picks a box at random and tosses it into the cart.

**EXT KNOXVILLE  JAMES HOUSE  FRONT YARD  LATE AFTERNOON  SOME DAYS LATER**

Rain water. Falling leaves. James is cleaning out the gutter, working under an overcast sky.

**INT KNOXVILLE JAMES HOUSE LIVING ROOM   EVENING**

James zones out in front of a snowy TV; the glow plays on his
face.

**INT KNOXVILLE   KITCHEN   NEXT MORNING**

Domesticity. Connie peels a pile of carrots. James washes
mushrooms in the sink.

He tries to clean them individually but they crumble in his
hands.

> JAMES
> Some guy drove his truck into a middle
> of an Iraqi market. He starts  passing
> out free candies. All the kids come
> running up - he detonates. (beat)
> They're saying fifty nine dead...

She's heard this kind of story before and knows where it ends.
She can't bring herself to reply.

> JAMES
> You know they need more bomb techs.

> CONNIE
> (handing James the
> carrots)
> Will you chop these up for me?

> JAMES PRELAP
> Boing! Boing! Boing!

**INT  JAMES' SON'S BEDROOM  LATER THAT NIGHT**

Bedtime. James is putting his son to sleep in a room decorated
with mobiles and colorful wall hangings. He sets the mobile
spinning.

> JAMES
> Boing! Boing!

The boy giggles and reaches up.

On the bed is a Jack-In-the-Box, which James picks up and winds.
He opens the toy for his son who squeals with delight, eyes wide
with admiration for his daddy. Daddy, however, isn't sure where
to go with this..An odd moment for the wild-man of Baghdad:
playing the awkward dad to his adoring child

James looks into his son's unconditionally loving eyes.

Something he sees there prompts a confession:

>                    JAMES
>          You love playing with that, don't
>          you..? You love all your stuffed
>          animals. You love your Mommy, your
>          Daddy. You love your pajamas... You
>          love everything, don't you?

James playfully spins the mobile. The boy laughs at the whirring color.

>                    JAMES
>          But you know what buddy, as you get
>          older some of the things that you love
>          might not seem so special anymore. You
>          know? Like your Jack-in-the-Box.

The boy touches the Jack-in-the-Box, smiling beautifully.

>                    JAMES
>          Maybe... you'll realize it's just a
>          piece of tin and a stuffed animal. And
>          the older you get, the fewer things
>          you really love.
>               (beat)
>          By the time you get to be my age,
>          maybe it's only one -- or two --
>          things.

James pauses. His son continues to giggle and play.

>                    JAMES
>          With me, I think it's one.

>                                        CUT TO:


**EXT  BAGHDAD  TARMAC**

--sonic overload of a C-130 airplane landing.

Wheels touch down on tarmac.


**INT EXT AIRPLANE**

The hydraulics of a loading ramp engage, lowering the ramp, and revealing a troop of young SOLDIERS inside the belly of the plane.

Passing over their frightened faces, we find one man who looks remarkably at ease.

James.

The soldiers disembark and we follow James as he leaves the plane and greets a another young EOD SOLDIER who has been waiting for him on the tarmac.

                    SOLDIER
          Welcome to Delta-Company.

James shakes his hand.

A Middle-Eastern sun bathes James' upturned face lengthening into a smile.

His pace slows...the tarmac *transitions* to dirt as little puffs of dust lift off his continuous passage.

*He is now in the bomb suit and we are --*

**EXT.  BAGHDAD OUTSKIRTS  DAY**

On yet another war-torn street.

Two fresh faced EOD SOLDIERS observe James as he makes another lonely walk down an empty block... heading to a bomb.

-- James' face glistening with pleasure

-- The noon day sun shimmers on his helmet shield

**TITLE:**

**DAYS LEFT IN DELTA COMPANY'S ROTATION: 365**

And we watch him go down the unnamed road until he disappears.

END

## TRUE FICTION: THE SCRIPT

In 2004, journalist and screenwriter Mark Boal spent weeks embedded with a U.S. Army bomb squad operating in one of the most dangerous sections of Baghdad. Their harrowing daily experiences led him to consider that the account of these young men who save lives and risk their own by disarming deadly bombs planted in population centers might best be appreciated in a fictional telling, set in that terrifyingly real world. When he returned from Iraq, Boal pitched the idea to filmmaker Kathryn Bigelow (*Point Break, Strange Days*), whom he had met when she was developing a television series based on an article he had written in 2002. The two decided to pursue the project independently, so as to limit a committee reaction to the tough material, and Boal went to work writing a 'spec' script.

"[The experience in Iraq] made a deep impression on me. When I got home, I thought, 'People have no idea how these guys live and what they're up against," says Boal, who also created the story for the drama *In the Valley of Elah*. "I was intrigued by the mental and psychological framework that a bomb technician develops on the job. What kind of personality is comfortable with extreme risk and with living so close to death? And in a thematic sense, the bomb squad seemed like a promising entry-point for a movie about the Iraq war."

During the early, bloodiest stages of the war, coalition bomb squads played a pivotal but mostly underreported part in the conflict. From 2004–2006, the Army relied on its bomb squads as the first—and last—line of defense against the IEDs [Improvised Explosive Devices] that had become the insurgency's weapon of choice. The opening scene in the movie depicts the kind of situation that U.S. soldiers in Baghdad encountered on a daily basis—sometimes ten or twenty times a day, according to Boal. "Army bomb technicians were thrust into a role that they had never played before in any other war.

And they quickly became the key strategic unit in the attempt to stem the growing tide of roadside bombs that were turning the city into an incredibly lethal, unpredictable, and insane environment."

# IN THE KILL ZONE: CHARACTERS AND CAST

At the core of *The Hurt Locker* are its characters. Against the deadly backdrop of twenty-first-century counter-insurgency warfare, Sergeant James becomes the heart of the story—a mercurial, swaggering, expert bomb technician who shocks his new team members with his enthusiastic disregard for established procedures. "Staff Sergeant James really anchors the movie; he's the galvanizing center of the team in that he instills both fear and admiration," says Kathryn Bigelow. "A lot of what happens in terms of character development is about how the other guys react to this almost elemental force that comes whirling into their already on-edge lives."

When it came to casting the film's three leads, Bigelow wanted to find breakout, young actors in order to heighten the film's authenticity and boost its surprise factor—avoiding the calming familiarity of an established movie star. "There's a convention that the movie star doesn't die until the end of a film, and I think that in our case having that certainty would undermine the naturally suspenseful, unpredictable quality of being in a war where death can happen anytime, to anyone," explains Bigelow. "With *The Hurt Locker*, I wanted it to be as tense and real as possible, and that meant having actors who were relatively fresh faces so the audience wouldn't know who among the three main characters was going to live or die by virtue of their public profile."

In considering who might play Staff Sergeant James, Bigelow conducted an exhaustive search of up-and-coming young talent before finding an actor with the range to realize the role of the wild, alluring, good old boy with a surprisingly rich interior life. The search ended when Jeremy Renner came to her attention via his turn playing the notorious title character in the film *Dahmer*.

James is the catalyst for much of the film's conflict. "His solitary focus is on the bomb," says Boal. "That's where he gets his engagement and his sense of being alive. He's most at home when he's working on a bomb and most out of place when he's just with other people. So in a sense, the price of his heroism is his isolation, or loneliness, and his inability to connect with other people who are close to him. His heroism is a flight from intimacy."

Jeremy Renner, who grew up in rural California, identified with the character's salt-of-the-earth background, and he was also drawn to a universal quality in the script that transcends its immediate setting. "What attracted me to it was the complexity of the character. He's not another clichéd, gung-ho soldier," Renner says.

Casting the role of Sergeant J.T. Sanborn—the proud, affable, level-headed intelligence specialist who has the toughness to go toe to toe with James—posed its own special challenges, recalls Bigelow. Anthony Mackie caught Bigelow's eye during his performances in *We Are Marshall, Million Dollar Baby,* and especially in his role as a menacing drug dealer in *Half Nelson,* opposite Ryan Gosling.

For his part, Mackie was attracted to the depth he saw in Sanborn's character, which allowed him to find many levels on which to play. "Sanborn hides behind his *machismo*," says Mackie. "There has to be a kind of superhero aspect to these soldiers. If they wake up every day in fear that every minute is the last, they'll drive themselves crazy. Down deep though, he's very humble."

In contrast to James' consuming passion for his work, Sergeant J. T. Sanborn is the film's Everyman. "He spent seven years in intelligence before joining EOD," says Boal. "He's a smart, capable, reliable, charismatic guy who has never encountered a whirlwind like James before. There's an alpha male component to his personality that runs up pretty hard against James, who's also an alpha male but of a much different stripe, so you have these two versions of masculinity dueling each other as they fight in these really tricky circumstances in Baghdad."

Providing the third side of the film's interpersonal triangle is Specialist Owen Eldridge, the youthful junior member of the team, who is in search of a mentor and who tries but ultimately fails to find solace in either Sanborn's stoicism or in James' indifference to danger. As the pain of the war creeps up on the young soldier, darkening his innocence, "Eldridge has to be every mother's son," explains Bigelow, "There's a frankness and earnestness to him that allows him to wear his fear on his sleeve." Bigelow had been impressed with Brian Geraghty's performances in *Jarhead, We Are Marshall,* and *Bobby* before she cast him as Eldridge in this film.

With the three leads in place, the next role to cast was Sergeant Matt Thompson, the team leader beloved by his teammates, who opens the movie. "We needed an actor who could immediately convey the ease of command and warmth with his men that good sergeants possess," explains Bigelow. The director's first choice was Guy Pearce, admired for his performances in *L.A. Confidential, Memento,* and *The Proposition.* "Having Guy open the film sets up a sense of credible reality from the very start," says Bigelow. "You need that because the world is so exotic, but Guy just seems like he belongs in it."

"I've wanted to work with Kathryn for years," says Pearce. "And ultimately the material has to be the reason why I go and do any film. This film is packed with action, but it's about people and emotions. It's about people trying to connect with each other. The way in which the script was written is really fascinating, and Mark and Kathryn have both done a beautiful job of capturing and realizing these characters."

Bigelow's reputation for eliciting strong performances from her actors attracted some big Hollywood guns who were willing to take on some of the film's more intriguing cameo roles, including David Morse, Ralph Fiennes, and Evangeline Lilly. Morse was electrified by the script's picture of a world that is completely unpredictable and dangerous. "It doesn't care who you are," he says. "Anybody can go at any time. There's a surreal quality to it. I think that says what the experience in Iraq is about."

## A REALIST EYE: THE PRODUCTION

For *The Hurt Locker*, Bigelow took her cast and crew into the Jordanian desert to work under some of the most rigorous conditions possible. With director of photography Barry Ackroyd, she devised an unconventional technique for filming that simulates the spontaneous feeling of a documentary, while immersing viewers in the nonstop tension of its characters' world.

Since his early days in documentary filmmaking, Ackroyd has refined his in-the-moment style in award-winning feature films, including *United 93*. "Making a feature film is not a documentary and it's not docudrama," he says. "The essence is not to think about it too much, but to try to be surprised in the way that a documentary would surprise you. Yes, we can set things up and we can redo it, but it's still possible to be surprised when the performance happens."

Bigelow made the choice to film *The Hurt Locker* with four handheld cameras simultaneously. She has shot with multiple cameras on each of her films, using as many as twelve at a time. "When I storyboard the entire film, every scene is broken down to its essential elements," she says (see samples pages 120-121). "I look at the boards shot by shot. It's at this point that I realize what the technical needs of the shoot are. I can determine the camera needs, as well as the blocking of each scene. Even before we've chosen locations, I have basically 'shot' the entire film in my head."

To meet an ambitious schedule of shooting *The Hurt Locker's* many extended action sequences in only forty-four days, the crew worked six-day weeks and blitzed through complicated, highly choreographed blocking that Bigelow would outline in her head well in advance. "I look at each sequence like a three-dimensional puzzle that has to be translated to a two-dimensional surface," she says.

It all starts with the script, she says. "In this case, it was the logic of bomb disarmament. Early on, I realized geography would be central to the audience's understanding of what the bomb squad does on a daily basis. Military protocol for a bomb disarm in the field is approximately a 300-meter containment. That's a big set."

On *The Hurt Locker*, the filmmakers used multiple points of view and constantly moving cameras to create the kind of immediacy that places the viewer in the center of the fog of war. "We were always asking ourselves, 'What can you do with the camera that can make you feel like you're a participant?'" says Ackroyd. "How do you put yourself in the middle of the scene or put yourself right on the edge of the scene and participate in what goes on? You can give the actors the space to do long takes with continuous action. The art department gave us big sets for the explosions. People were doing their stunts as big long takes and the camera was just participating in it. You don't ever stop; you just keep going with it. Kathryn gave us the space to do that. She said go ahead and keep shooting, keep shooting, keep shooting. We would be waiting for 'cut' sometimes and it wouldn't be coming, so we knew the shot was working well."

"We had cameras everywhere," says Renner. "We called them Ninja cameras, just hiding all over the place. We never knew where anything was. Barry was out there himself running around. It was absolutely amazing seeing him run as fast as we did, carrying his camera down these dirty alleys

# STORYBOARDS: OPENING SEQUENCE

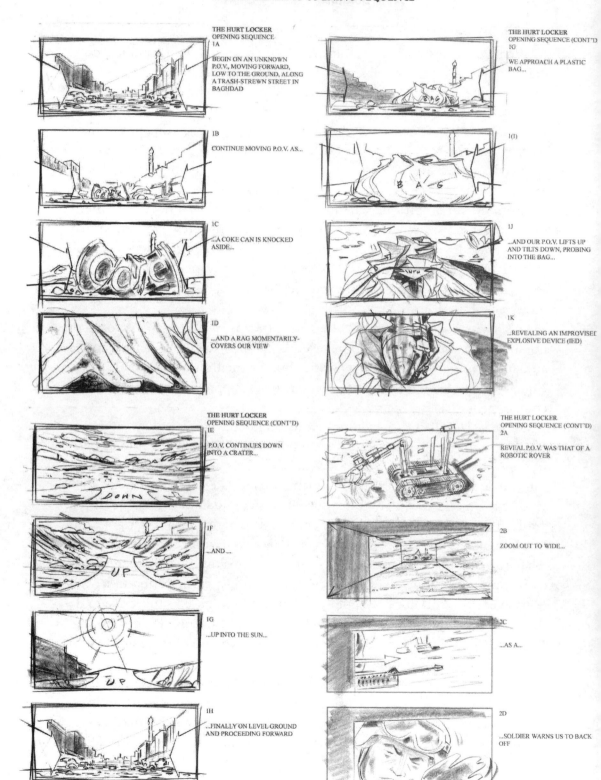

THE HURT LOCKER
OPENING SEQUENCE
1A

BEGIN ON AN UNKNOWN
P.O.V., MOVING FORWARD,
LOW TO THE GROUND, ALONG
A TRASH-STREWN STREET IN
BAGHDAD

1B

CONTINUE MOVING P.O.V. AS...

1C

...A COKE CAN IS KNOCKED
ASIDE...

1D

...AND A RAG MOMENTARILY-
COVERS OUR VIEW

THE HURT LOCKER
OPENING SEQUENCE (CONT'D)
1E

P.O.V. CONTINUES DOWN
INTO A CRATER...

1F

...AND ...

1G

...UP INTO THE SUN...

1H

...FINALLY ON LEVEL GROUND
AND PROCEEDING FORWARD

THE HURT LOCKER
OPENING SEQUENCE (CONT'D)
1G

WE APPROACH A PLASTIC
BAG...

1(I)

1J

...AND OUR P.O.V. LIFTS UP
AND TILTS DOWN, PROBING
INTO THE BAG...

1K

...REVEALING AN IMPROVISED
EXPLOSIVE DEVICE (IED)

THE HURT LOCKER
OPENING SEQUENCE (CONT'D)
2A

REVEAL P.O.V. WAS THAT OF A
ROBOTIC ROVER

2B

ZOOM OUT TO WIDE...

2C

...AS A...

2D

...SOLDIER WARNS US TO BACK
OFF

120

# STORYBOARDS: JAMES DEBUT SEQUENCE

THE HURT LOCKER
JAMES' DEBUT (CONT'D)

95

O.T.S. JAMES AS HE CLIPS THE WIRES

96

AT THE SAME TIME, THE MAN IN THE BUSINESS SUIT DESCENDS A FLIGHT OF STAIRS

97

JAMES LIFTS THE DEFUSED DEVICE...

98

...AND STANDS

J.: "We're done."

THE HURT LOCKER
JAMES' DEBUT (CONT'D)

99

PUSH INTO JAMES AS HE SEES...

100

JAMES P.O.V.

...ANOTHER WIRE

101

J.: (O.S.) "Secondary!"

102

JAMES STARTS TO PULL THE WIRE UP

THE HURT LOCKER
JAMES' DEBUT (CONT'D)

103

THE MAN IN THE BUSINESS SUIT EXITS HIS BUILDING

104

JAMES TAKES NOTE

105

THE MAN LOOKS AROUND

106

HE SEEMS TO LOOK TOWARD A TELEPHONE POLE WHERE THERE IS A SMALL BUTTON-BOX AND A WIRE LEADING TO THE GROUND

THE HURT LOCKER
JAMES' DEBUT (CONT'D)

107

JAMES CONTINUES TO PULL THE WIRE UP AND DISCOVERS...

108

...THE WIRES BRANCH OUT...

109

JAMES REALIZES HE'S...

110

...SURROUNDED BY A WEB OF EXPLOSIVES!

121

full of syringes and kids throwing rocks, and he always had a big smile on his face. That inspired me."

Shooting in this way required flexibility on the part of the actors. "There was only so much you could prepare for," says Geraghty. "But if you've done your homework and you know your character, all that stuff falls into place and you can just put your trust in it. There are so many technical things outside of your performance. Lights, camera, heat, camels, goats—you have to just keep going."

Ackroyd also used the camerawork to punctuate the often frenzied activity with moments of quiet. "Kathryn encouraged the cameras to be active," he says. "I was always thinking about the moments of stillness that you have as well and how those things go together. If those things come together in the right way, motion is one dimension, and silence and lack of motion add another element. If you get those things right, the whole film will have balance."

In order to simulate the troubled landscape of war-torn Baghdad, Bigelow decided to film in Jordan, which borders Iraq to the west. Some of the locations were just a few hours drive from the combat areas. "It adds a certain x-factor that just permeates every aspect of the performance and the production to be that close," says Bigelow, "and it becomes part of your reference points if you actually spend time off set within an Arabic culture."

The production took place in and around the poorer neighborhoods in the city of Amman, which had architecture similar to Baghdad's. The climate and geography of the two countries are also comparable, with the added bonus of the presence of ethnic Iraqis who could fill small parts and work as background and bit players, further heightening the realism of the film.

"There are about one million Iraqi refugees living in Jordan who have fled the war, and as it turns out, among them is a pretty big pool of professional actors, and it was great to be able to cast them—it was good for the movie, and it was good for the set," explains Bigelow.

The desire for authenticity extended to the actor's living arrangements as well. In order to instill the military's close camaraderie, Bigelow housed all the actors on set in a basic communal tent with a dirt floor, rather than in air-conditioned trailers. Before the shoot, Renner, Geraghty, and the other principals spent time learning from Army EOD teams at the National Training

Center at Fort Irwin. Located near Barstow, California, the NTC is the army's premier training camp. Its Mojave Desert location makes it perfect for instructing troops headed for the Middle East. "It's just crazy," says Geraghty. "When there's a bomb, most people want get as far away from it as possible. These guys are trained to do the opposite. Their job is to go in as close as they can get."

What cast and filmmakers remember most about shooting in Jordan was the summer heat. "There was something incredibly immediate about shooting in an environment that was unforgivably hot and putting the actors in a very arduous situation on a day to day basis," says Bigelow. "Just sand, wind, sand, heat, sun and sand."

Not surprisingly, the actors found the conditions challenging. "It would be 105, 110 degrees," says Mackie. "It was so hot you could feel your brain cooking in your head. Everything was magnified by the level of body armor we had to wear."

Renner adds: "Working in Jordan was extremely difficult in the sense that conditions were very hard. But it made my job as an actor easier. That sweat is real sweat. Those tears are real tears of pain, so I'm glad we weren't on some soundstage. I feel like I got just a sliver of an idea of what an EOD or anybody in the military might go through every day. It's unbelievable how torturous it can be.

"It was the hardest thing I've had to do physically as an actor," he continues. "I love to be challenged, and I was really, really challenged on this. I think we all had a nervous breakdown or two or three—I kept telling my mom to FedEx my dignity back to me. But the most awful days I had were the most memorable. I look back and I know it was the most spectacular experience that I've had as a man, not even just as an actor."

Boal's on-the-ground experiences as a journalist in Iraq familiarized him with the specifics of EOD operations, such as the procedure the team leader follows to put on the protective suit. "There is a whole ritual to unpacking the suit," says Boal. "Getting into the suit signifies the moment when the war becomes a solitary encounter between one man and a deadly device that's been created with the express intention of causing harm. Once the team leader is in it, there's no going back. He faces that lonely walk down to the bomb, and it's just him and this suit."

Made of Kevlar fabric with ceramic plates, the suit is designed to protect the wearer from the impact of a blast, but it cannot withstand the largest explosions. "We thought of it like a suit of armor that a knight would wear in medieval times," says Boal. "They have to put it on, because it's the only thing they have, but it certainly doesn't offer foolproof protection from the enemy."

Renner spent significant time wearing the suit for his role. "My feelings about the bomb suit are mixed," he says. "You're definitely alone once you get into it, but there's something really peaceful about that. I felt like that was a womb for James. That's the only time when he really felt safe, as a human being, not just as a soldier."

Once the movie moved into post-production, sound designer Paul Ottoson, who was nominated for an Academy Award for his work on *Spiderman 2*, went to work layering in the thousands of sounds that sound mixer Ray Beckett had recorded in Jordan. "From a sound perspective, this movie was incredibly difficult and unusual, definitely the hardest I ever worked on, because the score was very spare and ambient and there was so much detail in the sound. Practically every frame of the movie has a sound attached to it—it's wall-to-wall sound—to give you that feeling that you are in a real war," says Ottoson. "Every single sound of the movie is an organic base to it. We didn't use any synthetic sounds because they are kind of unnatural, thin, slicing sounds. It is easier to get synthetic sounds to be loud. Staying organic the entire movie was difficult but we did it, because in the end it helped tell the story best."

# U.S. ARMY EXPLOSIVE ORDNANCE DISPOSAL: FAST FACTS

In 2004, there were only about 150 trained Army EOD techs in Iraq.

The job was so dangerous that EOD techs were five times more likely to die than all other soldiers in the theater. That same year, the insurgency reportedly placed a $25,000 bounty on the heads of EOD techs.

Bomb shrapnel travels at 2,700 feet per second. Overpressure, the deadly wave of super-compressed gases that expands from the center of a blast, travels at 13,000 miles an hour—at a force equal to 700 tons per square inch.

Separations and relationship troubles are so common among EOD teams that soldiers sometimes joke that EOD stands for "every one divorced."

Bomb-disposal teams were first created in World War II. Starting in 1942, when Germany blitzed London with time-delayed bombs, specially trained U.S. soldiers joined British officers, who diagrammed the devices using pencil sketches before they attempted to defuse them with common tools.

Bomb techs are trained at Eglin Air Force Base in Florida. The Army looks for volunteers who are confident, forthright, comfortable under extreme pressure, and emotionally stable. To get into the training program, a prospective tech first needs a high score on the mechanical-aptitude portion of the armed forces exam. Once the school begins, candidates are gradually winnowed out over six months of training, and only 40 percent will graduate.

# CAST AND CREW CREDITS

SUMMIT ENTERTAINMENT PRESENTS IN ASSOCIATION WITH
VOLTAGE PICTURES AND GROSVENOR PARK MEDIA, LP AND F.C.S.A.
A VOLTAGE PICTURES/FIRST LIGHT/KINGSGATE FILMS PRODUCTION
OF A KATHRYN BIGELOW FILM

## "THE HURT LOCKER"

JEREMY RENNER   ANTHONY MACKIE   BRIAN GERAGHTY   EVANGELINE LILLY
WITH   RALPH FIENNES   DAVID MORSE   AND   GUY PEARCE

| | | |
|---|---|---|
| Casting by<br>MARK BENNETT | Costume Designer<br>GEORGE LITTLE | Executive Producer<br>TONY MARK |
| Music by<br>MARCO BELTRAMI AND<br>BUCK SANDERS | Sound Design by<br>PAUL N.J. OTTOSSON | Produced by<br>KATHRYN BIGELOW  MARK<br>BOAL  NICOLAS CHARTIER<br>GREG SHAPIRO |
| Music Supervisor<br>JOHN BISSELL | Editors<br>BOB MURAWSKI<br>CHRIS INNIS | Written by<br>MARK BOAL |
| Production Designer<br>KARL JÚLÍUSSON | Director of Photography<br>BARRY ACKROYD, BSC | Directed by<br>KATHRYN BIGELOW |

### CAST

STAFF SERGEANT WILLIAM JAMES
. . . . . . . . . . . . . JEREMY RENNER
SERGEANT JT SANBORN
. . . . . . . . . . . ANTHONY MACKIE
SPECIALIST OWEN ELDRIDGE
. . . . . . . . . . . BRIAN GERAGHTY
SERGEANT MATT THOMPSON
. . . . . . . . . . . . . GUY PEARCE
CONTRACTOR TEAM LEADER
. . . . . . . . . . . . RALPH FIENNES
COLONEL REED . . . . . DAVID MORSE
CONNIE JAMES . . . EVANGELINE LILLY
COLONEL JOHN CAMBRIDGE
. . . . . . . . . . CHRISTIAN CAMARGO
BLACK SUIT MAN
. . . . . . . . . . SUHAIL AL-DABBACH
BECKHAM . . . CHRISTOPHER SAYEGH
PROFESSOR NABIL . . . . . NABIL KONI
CONTRACTOR CHARLIE
. . . . . . . . . . . . . SAM SPRUELL
CONTRACTOR JIMMY
. . . . . . . . . . . . . SAM REDFORD
CONTRACTOR FEISAL
. . . . . . . . . . . . FEISAL SADOUN
CONTRACTOR CHRIS . . BARRIE RICE

IRAQI POLICE CAPTAIN AT UN
. . . . . . . . . . . . . IMAD DAOUDI
MORTUARY AFFAIRS OFFICER
. . . . . . . . . . . . . ERIN GANN
SERGEANT CARTER
. . . . . . . . . . JUSTIN CAMPBELL
SERGEANT FOSTER
. . . . . . . . . MALCOLM BARRETT
SOLDIER AT INTERSECTION
. . . . . . . . . KRISTOFFER WINTER
GUARD AT CAMP LIBERTY MARKET
. . . . . . . . . . . . . J. J. KANDEL
GUARD AT LIBERTY GATE
. . . . . . . . . . . RYAN TRAMONT
IRAQI TRANSLATOR
. . . . . . . . . . MICHAEL DESANTE
DVD MERCHANT . . . HASAN DARWISH
INSURGENT IN THE STAIRWELL
. . . . . . . . . . . . WASFI AMOUR
NABI L'S WIFE . . . . . NIBRAS QASSEM
US ARMY MEDIC . . . . . BEN THOMAS
INSURGENT SNIPER
. . . . . . . . . . . NADER TARAWNEH
SOLDIER AT UN
. . . . . . . . ANAS "TIPSY" WELLMAN
BUTCHER . . . . . . . . OMAR MARIO
SOLDIER AT AIRFIELD
. . . . . . . . . . FLEMING CAMPBELL

# CREW

UNIT PRODUCTION MANAGER
. . . . . . . . . . . . . . . . . TONY MARK
FIRST ASSISTANT DIRECTOR
. . . . . . . . . . . . . . . DAVID TICOTIN
SECOND ASSISTANT DIRECTOR
. . . . . . . . . . . . . . . NICK HARVARD

CO-PRODUCER
. . . . . . . . . . . DONALL MCCUSKER
ASSOCIATE PRODUCER
. . . . . . . . . . . . . JACK SCHUSTER
ASSOCIATE PRODUCER . . . . JENN LEE
PRODUCTION MANAGER
. . . . . . . . . . . . . KARIMA LADJIMI
PRODUCTION SUPERVISOR . J. GIBSON
ART DIRECTOR . . . . . . DAVID BRYAN
CAMERA OPERATORS
. . . . . . . . . . . SCOTT MCDONALD
                DURAID MUNAJIM
SPECIAL EFFECTS SUPERVISOR
. . . . . . . . . . RICHARD STUTSMAN
SET COSTUMER . . . . RICK DE SOUZA
FIRST ASSISTANT EDITOR
. . . . . . . . . . . . . . . SEAN VALLA
ASSISTANT PRODUCTION
COORDINATOR . . . . . ISSA SAWAQED
SCRIPT SUPERVISOR
. . . . . . . ASLAUG KONRADSDOTTIR
PRODUCTION CONSULTANT
. . . . . . . . . . . . . . . FUAD KHALIL
PRODUCTION SECRETARY
. . . . . . . . . . . . . . . MAJD HIJJAWI
SECOND ASSISTANT DIRECTOR
. . . . . . . . . . . . . YANAL BARAKAT
HI-SPEED CAMERA OPERATOR
. . . . . . DORY AOUN (THIRD EYE FX)
FIRST ASSISTANT CAMERA
. . . . . . . . . . . STEWART WHELAN
                OLIVER DRISCOLL
                IMAD RECHICHE
SECOND ASSISTANT CAMERA
. . . . . . . . . . . . . THOMAS TAYLOR
                GLENN COULMAN
                MOUNA KHAALI
CAMERA ASSISTANTS . . . BEISAN ELIAS
                TAMER NABER
                RUSSELL WEBER
KEY GRIP . . . . . . MHER KESHISHIAN
BEST BOY GRIP . . . . . . . ELIE MERHI
GRIPS . . . . . . . . . CHADY CHEHADE
                PRINCE KHOURY
                HUSNY BKHAA
VIDEO ASSIST OPERATOR

. . . . . . . . . . . . . . SAMI SEHWEIL
ASSISTANT VIDEO ASSISTS
. . . . . . . . . . . . . . ALI SHAHEEN
                AHMAD TAKARI
                ZEID NAWAFLEH
SOUND MIXER . . . . . . RAY BECKETT
BOOM OPERATOR . . . SIMON BYSSHE
ASSISTANT ART DIRECTOR
. . . . . . . . . . . . . NADEER IBRAHIM
STANDBY ASSISTANT ART DIRECTOR
. . . . . . . . . . . . . . SANA'A JABER
KEY SCENIC PAINTER
. . . . . . . . . . . . . SAMIR ZAIDAN
ASSISTANT SCENIC PAINTER
. . . . . . . . . . . . . RIME AL-JABER
STORYBOARD ARTIST
. . . . . . . . . . . . . . GARY THOMAS
SPECIAL EFFECTS FOREMEN
. . . . . . . . . . . . . . BLAIR FOORD
                ERNST GSCHWIND
SPECIAL EFFECTS TECHNICIANS
. . . . . . . . . . . . . . WOLF STEILING
                ERNST LANNINJER
SPECIAL EFFECTS PURCHASER
. . . . . . . . . . . . . RAFIQ KAMHAWI
SPECIAL EFFECTS IED CONSULTANT
. . . . . . . . . MOHAMMAD AL KURDI
SPECIAL EFFECTS TECHNICIAN,
JORDAN . . . . . . . HELMI ANADEEN
RE-RECORDING MIXER
. . . . . . . . . . . PAUL N. J. OTTOSSON
DIALOGUE/ADR EDITORS
. . . . . . . . . . . . . ROBERT TROY
                KIMBERLY HARRIS
SFX EDITORS . . . . . . . JAMIE HARDT
                BERNARD WEISER
                RICK FRANKLIN
FOLEY EDITORS . . . JOHN SANACORE
                ALEX ULLRICH
FIRST ASSISTANT SOUND EDITOR
. . . . . . . . . . . . . RYAN JUGGLER
ASSISTANT EDITOR . . . MICHAEL KAZ
ADR VOICE CASTING
. . . . . . . . . . . . . THE FINAL WORD
POST PRODUCTION SUPERVISOR
. . . . . . . . . . . . . JACK SCHUSTER
COSTUME SUPERVISOR
. . . . . . . . . . . . . . MOIRA MEYER
ASSISTANT COSTUME DESIGNERS
. . . . . . . . . . . . . DANIEL LESTER
                HANADI
ON-SET COSTUMERS . . . FADI OMEISH
                PHAEDRA DAHDALEH
COSTUMER BUYER . . KARMA HIJJAWI
COSTUME AGER . . . MELISSA BINDER

127

"SUIT" COSTUMER. . . . . . BLUE SOLE
WARDROBE ASSISTANTS
. . . . . . . . . ABED AL FATAH RAYAN
MOHAMED MAHSEERI
SET DECORATOR . . AMEEN AL-MASRI
SET DRESSERS . . . . . . . ZACHARIA
ASAD
HAIR AND MAKE-UP DESIGNER
. . . . . . . . . . . . . DANIEL PARKER
ASSISTANT HAIR AND MAKE-UP
DESIGNERS. . . . . ELIZABETH RAPLEY
YELKA GUTIERREZ
PROSTHETIC MAKE-UP ARTIST
. . . . . . . . . . ROBIN PRITCHARD
GAFFER . . . . . . MATTHEW MOFFATT

BEST BOY ELECTRIC
. . . . . . . . . . . OSAMA NAMROUQA
ELECTRICIANS
. . . . . . . . . . . . BASHIR MOUAWAD
ELIE BEAINO
FIRAS DIHOUS
BASSEL SLAYEBE
MELIK KHAZZOUM
ISSAM DOURY
GENERATOR OPERATOR
. . . . . . . . . . HAMMADA EL BAKA
PROPERTY MASTER . . . . MIKE MALIK
ASSISTANT PROP MASTER
. . . . . . . . . . . . . KARIM KHEIR
STANDBY PROPS . . . . NASSER ZOUBI
FARIS ZIYOUD
WEAPONS SPECIALIST . . DAVID FENCL
WEAPONS ASSISTANT . . KHALIL HARB
ROBOT TECHNICIAN. . CHRIS SURBER
CONSTRUCTION COORDINATOR
. . . . . . . . . . . . MARWAN KHEIR
PRODUCTION ACCOUNTANT
. . . . . . . . . . . DEBBIE CHESEBRO
FIRST ASSISTANT ACCOUNTANT
. . . . . . . . . . . . MARK HOUSTON
SECOND ASSISTANT ACCOUNTANT
. . . . . . . . . . . DEBBIE PETERSEN
STIL LS PHOTOGRAPHER
. . . . . . . . . . . . JONATHAN OLLEY
JORDAN PUBLICITY . . . ISSA MATALKA
TRAVEL COORDINATOR
. . . . . . . . . . . . . IMAD DAOUDI
LOCATION MANAGER. . FAWAZ ZOUBI
ASSISTANT LOCATION MANAGER
. . . . . . . . . . . . . HAITHAM KAYED
LOCATIONS ASSISTANTS
. . . . . MOHAMED (GABA) NAWAFLEH
ALI AL KHALAILEH
JORDAN CASTING . . . . LARA ATALLA

EXTRAS COORDINATOR
. . . . . . . . . . . . . SETENAY ISHAK
EDITORIAL ASSISTANT
. . . . . . . . . . . . . RUPERT LLOYD
UK FILM RUNNER . . . DAVID MORRIS
ASSISTANT TO MS. BIGELOW
. . . . . . . . . . . . . JOHN R. SCOTT
ASSISTANT TO MR. BOAL
. . . . . . . . . . . . OMAR HABIBB
ASSISTANT TO MR. CHARTIER
. . . . . . . . . . . . . ANDREA BALL
ASSISTANT TO MR. MARK
. . . . . . . . . . . . LARA SAWALHA
PRODUCTION ASSISTANTS
. . . . . . . . . . . YAHYA SHAHEEN
BADER ALAMI
BASSEL GHANDOUR
OMAR SWALHA
RAYA QARAEIN
MOHAMED JAWAD
THERESA GUNTLI
PRODUCTION RUNNERS. . ZIAD FARAJ
ZEID DARWAZEH
MILITARY ADVISOR
. . . . . . . . . CSM JAMES CLIFFORD,
USA/EOD(RETIRED)
TECHNICAL CONSULTANTS
. . . . . . . . . . . . . BEN THOMAS
BARRIE RICE
MATTHEW THOMPSON
JORDANIAN MILITARY LIAISON
. . . . . . . . . . . MARWAN ABADI

STUNTS
STUNT COORDINATOR
. . . . . . . . . . . . ROBERT YOUNG
STUNT CO-COORDINATOR
. . . . . . . . . . . . . . BARRIE RICE
STUNT PERFORMERS
. . . . . . . . . . . . ANTONIO MARSH
ISAAC HAMON
TRANSPORTATION MANAGER
. . . . . . . . . . . MAHDI NAWAFLEH
JORDANIAN PRODUCTION SERVICES
. . . . . . . SANDBAG PRODUCTIONS

SECOND UNIT
DIRECTOR OF PHOTOGRAPHY
. . . . . . . NIELS REEDTZ JOHANSEN
FIRST ASSISTANT CAMERA
. . . . . . . . . . . . RUSSELL KENNEDY
SECOND ASSISTANT CAMERA
. . . . . . . . . . . . MAX GLICKMAN
COORDINATOR . . . . ASHRAF ASA'AD
CAMERA PA . . . . . ABDEL SALAM HAJJ

128

CANADIAN UNIT
CANADIAN PRODUCTION SERVICES
. . . . . . . . . . INSIGHT FILM STUDIOS
ASSOCIATE PRODUCER . . KIRK SHAW
DIRECTOR OF PHOTOGRAPHY
. . . . . . . . . . . . . . . TOM SIGEL, ASC
PRODUCTION MANAGER
. . . . . . . . . . . . . . . . . ROB LYCAR
FIRST ASSISTANT DIRECTOR
. . . . . . . . . . . . . . . . LEE CLEARY
SECOND ASSISTANT DIRECTOR
. . . . . . . . . MICHELLE FITZPATRICK
PRODUCTION COORDINATORS
. . . . . . . . . . . MICAH GARDENER
                          JIM MCKEOWN
CASTING . . LAURA BROOKE TOPLASS
SCRIPT SUPERVISOR . . . . ANA SEBAL
PRODUCTION SOUND MIXER
. . . . . . . . . . . . . CRAIG STAUFFER
BOOM OPERATOR
. . . . . . . . . . . . . JUNIPER WATTERS
THIRD ASSISTANT DIRECTOR
. . . . . . . . . . . . . . . . ASHLEY BELL
TRAINEE ASSISTANT DIRECTOR
. . . . . . . . . . . . . . DALE BREDESON
COSTUME DESIGNER
. . . . . . . . . . . VICKI MULHOLLAND
PRODUCTION DESIGNER
. . . . . . . . . . . . . . . PAUL JOYAL
SET SUPERVISOR
. . . . . . . . . . SARA RAKHSHANDEF
SET DECORATOR . . IAN NOTHNAGEL
ON-SET DRESSER . . . SPENCER WEST
KEY MAKE-UP ARTIST
. . . . . . . . DANA MICHELLE HAMEL
KEY HAIR STYLIST . . JANICE RHODES
PROPS MASTER. . . . . DAVID INKSTER
FIRST ASSISTANT A CAMERA
. . . . . . . . . . . . . DAVID LOURIE
SECOND ASSISTANT A CAMERA
. . . . . . . . . . . . JEREMY SPOFFORD
B CAMERA OPERATOR
. . . . . . . . . . . . . . DALE JAHRAUS
FIRST ASSISTANT B CAMERA
. . . . . . . . . . . . . . ROBIN SMITH
SECOND ASSISTANT B CAMERA
. . . . . . . . . . . . . . ANDY CAPICIK
LOADER . . . . . . ROBERT FINNIGAN
STILLS PHOTOGRAPHER
. . . . . . . . . . . . . . ED ARAQUEL
LOCATIONS MANAGER. . . JAMIE LAKE
SCOUT . . . . . . . CAMPBELL SWEENY
KEY GRIP . . DAVE "BUCKET" WALKER
BEST BOY GRIP . . . KRIS GRUNEWALD
DOLLY GRIP . . . . . . . JULES QUESNEL

GAFFER . . . . . . . . . . JIM SWANSON
BEST BOY ELECTRIC . . . GEOFF DANE
BUSINESS AFFAIRS. . BREANNE HARTLEY
                SHANNON MCA'NULTY
PRODUCTION COUNSEL
. . . . . . . . . . . DORAN CHANDLER
                   (ROBERTS & STAHL)
PRODUCTION ACCOUNTANT
. . . . . . . . . . . . . KAREN AUSTIN
PAYROLL ACCOUNTANT
. . . . . . . . . . . . LEAH TANAFRANCA
CATERING OPERATOR
. . . . . . . . . . . NIN RAI (TRUFFLES)
CRAFT SERVICES/ FIRST AID
. . . . . . . . . . . . RODOLFO SCALI
TRANSPORTATION COORDINATOR
. . . . . . . . . . . DEAN FITZPATRICK
SECURITY CAPTAIN
. . . . . . . . . . . . DARREN HOWARD
DIGITAL INTERMEDIATE & VISUAL
EFFECTS PROVIDED BY . . COMPANY 3
CO3 EXECUTIVE PRODUCER
. . . . . . . . . . STEFAN SONNENFELD
COLORIST. . . . STEPHEN NAKAMURA
DI PRODUCER . . . . . ERIK ROGERS
ON-LINE EDITOR/VFX ARTIST
. . . . . . . . . . . ALEX ROMANO
DI TECHNOLOGIST . . . MIKE CHIADO
HEAD OF PRODUCTION
. . . . . . . . . . . . . BRUCE LOMET
VP, FEATURE SALES. . . . . JACKIE LEE
DI SCANNING SUPERVISOR
. . . . . . . . . . . . MICHAEL BOGGS
DI SCANNER . . . . . . . IAN TURPEN
DIGITAL DIRT REMOVAL
. . . . . . . . . MICHAEL CORONADO
DI ASSISTANTS . . JAMES CODY BAKER
                   JEREMIAH MOREY
TITLES BY . . . . . . SCARLET LETTERS

VFX
CGI SUPERVISOR . . . . . MITCH GATES
VISUAL EFFECTS PRODUCER
. . . . . . . . . . . . TOM KENDALL
VISUAL EFFECTS ARTISTS
. . . . . . . . . . . GAVIN MILJKOVICH
                    DAVE NEUBERGER
                    R. EDWARD BLACK
                    DOUG SPILATRO
CG ARTISTS . . . . . . . . . DAN LOPEZ
                    KURT MCKEEVER
                    CHANGSOO EUN
                    RODRIGO WASHINGTON
I/O DATA MANAGEMENT
. . . . . . . . . . . DAVID CAMARENA

129

INSURANCE. . AON/ALBERT G. RUBEN
            INSURANCE SERVICES, INC.
LEGAL SERVICES BY. . EISNER & FRANK
PRODUCT PLACEMENT BY
. . . . . . . . . . STONE MANAGEMENT
PRODUCT PLACEMENT
COORDINATORS . . . . . ADAM STONE
                        CAT STONE
PAYROLL COMPANY
. . . . . . ENTERTAINMENT PARTNERS
COLLECTION ACCOUNT
MANAGEMENT BY. . FINTAGE CAM B.V.
CAMERAS & LENSES BY. . . . ICE FILMS
FILM STOCK BY . . . . . . FUJI LONDON
                        KODAK
GRIP/ELECTRIC EQUIPMENT
. . . . . . . . . . . TELEMAX/PLATFORM
LAB FACILITIES BY . . . . SOHO IMAGES
TELECINE BY . . . . . . SOHO IMAGES
DELUXE LABS COLOR TIMER
. . . . . . . . . . . GILBERT CARRERAS
FINANCING PROVIDED BY
. . . . . . GROSVENOR PARK MEDIA, LP
COMPLETION GUARANTY PROVIDED
BY. . . . . CINEFINANCE INSURANCE
                        SERVICES, LLC
U.S. MILITARY EQUIPMENT
PROVIDED BY . . . . CHARLES TAYLOR
        MOVIE ARMAMENTS GROUP
PROSTHETICS BY. . ANIMATED EXTRAS
CRAFT SERVICES . . . . . . FADI SARAF
CATERING
. . . . ASKADENIA CATERING SERVICES
        NATIONAL FOOD COMPANY
EPK BY . . . . . . . . . . . CHRIS BOAL
EPK ASSISTANT . . . . AMER AL DWEIK
SECURITY . . . . . . . . BARRIE RICE

MUSIC
MUSIC SUPERVISOR . . . JOHN BISSELL
MUSIC COORDINATOR
. . . . . . . . . . . . . SARAH FERGUSON
MUSIC EDITOR . . . . . . JULIE PEARCE
MUSIC BY. . . MARCO BELTRAMI AND
                        BUCK SANDERS
MUSIC PREPARATION BY
. . . . . JOANN KANE MUSIC SERVICES
GUITAR PERFORMED BY
. . . . . . . . . . . . . BUCK SANDERS
VIOLIN PERFORMED BY
. . . . . . . . . . . . . ENDRE GRANAT
CELLO PERFORMED BY
. . . . . . . . . . . . ANDREW SHULMAN
BASS PERFORMED BY. . MIKE VALERIO
ERHU PERFORMED BY . . KAREN HAN

VOICE AND ETHNIC INSTRUMENTS
PERFORMED BY . . . YORGOS ADAMIS
MUSICIANS CONTRACTED BY
. . . . . . . . . . . . . PETER ROTTER
MUSIC MIXED BY. . JOHN KURLANDER

SONGS
"FEAR (IS BIG BUSINESS)"
WRITTEN BY JOURGENSEN / VICTOR
/ MINISTRY
PERFORMED BY MINISTRY
COURTESY OF 13TH PLANET
RECORDS, INC.

"PALESTINA"
WRITTEN BY JOURGENSEN / VICTOR
/ MINISTRY
PERFORMED BY MINISTRY
COURTESY OF 13TH PLANET
RECORDS, INC.

"YOUR SMILING FACE"
WRITTEN BY NORMAN CANDLER
PERFORMED BY
THE NORMAN CANDLER STRINGS
COURTESY OF APM MUSIC

"KHYBER PASS"
WRITTEN BY JOURGENSEN /
MINISTRY/ RAVEN / VICTOR
PERFORMED BY MINISTRY
COURTESY OF 13TH PLANET
RECORDS, INC.

SPECIAL THANKS TO
HIS MAJESTY KING ABDULLAH I I OF
JORDAN
HIS ROYAL HIGHNESS PRINCE ALI AL
HUSSEIN
HIS ROYAL HIGHNESS PRINCE HUSSEIN
NASSER MIRZA
HER ROYAL HIGHNESS PRINCESS RYM
AL ALI
HIS EXCELLENCY AMBASSADOR
TIMOOR GHAZI DAGHISTANI
FEISAL SADOUN
ROYAL JORDANIAN FILM COMMISSION
GEORGE DAVID
NADER TARAWNEH
FADI SARAF
EF SOLUTIONS, LLC
NORTHROP GRUMMAN
CORPORATION
PAUL C. CABELLON
MED-ENG

JOHN EAREY
REMOTEC, INC.
MARK KAUCHAK
JIM DANIELS
ROYCE HOLLMAN

PRODUCERS ALSO WISH TO THANK
MIKE ADLER
CHRIS ANDREWS
BONNIE BERNSTEIN
JIMMY DE BRABANT
NADINE DE BARROS
SIMON BERESFORD
STEVEN BROOKMAN
SANDRA BENOIT
SPENCER BAUMGARTEN
JOE COHEN
ANN DUVAL
CRAIG EMANUEL
JAMIE FELDMAN
IRENE FLORES
DARIN FRANK
BETH HOLDEN GARLAND
MATTHEW GABIN
DIANE GOLDEN
RICHARD GOLDSTEIN

SPIKE HOOPER
CAROLYN HUNT
ERIK HYMAN
STEVEN CHARLES JAFFE
PERRY KIPPERMAN
JOHN LOGAN
BOB LOVE
JOEL LUBIN
KOOL MARDER
CHUCK MARSHALL
HARRIS MASLANSKY
ALISSA MILLER
FRED MILSTEIN
ROBERT OFFER
DEIRDRE OWENS
HYLDA QUEALLY
EILEEN RAPKE
ELIZABETH RIAL
LEE ROSENBAUM

WILLIAM SEERY
RUSSEL SHATTLES
BRIAN SIBERELL
MEAGHAN SILVERMAN
BRAD SMALL
LEE SOLOMON
CHRISTIAN HALSEY
SOLOMON

JASON SPIRE
DONALD STARR
DONALD W. STEELE
MIMI STEINBAUER
KEN STOVITZ
ERIC SUDDLESON
ROEG SUTHERLAND
DARREN TRATTNER
DAVID WEBER
SALLY WILLCOX
STEPHEN ZAGER

5.11 TACTICAL
AMREL
ANHEUSER-BUSCH
APPLE
ASP, INC.
BENCHMADE

BRIGADE QUARTERMASTERS
CYALUME
DOCKERS
ESS
LEATHERMAN TOOL GROUP

MECHANIX
MOTORTABS
OAKLEY
PEPSI
PUMA
UNDER ARMOUR

FILMED ON LOCATION IN JORDAN
AND IN VANCOUVER, BRITISH
COLUMBIA

DISTRIBUTED BY SUMMIT DISTRIBUTION,
LLC

# About the Filmmakers

**MARK BOAL** (Writer and Producer) is a journalist, screenwriter, and producer. Born and raised in New York City, he graduated with honors in philosophy from Oberlin College before beginning a career as an investigative reporter and writer of long form nonfiction. An acclaimed series for the *Village Voice* on the rise of surveillance in America led to a position at the alternative weekly writing a weekly column, "The Monitor," when he was 23. Boal subsequently covered politics, technology, crime, youth culture, and drug culture in stories for a variety of national publications including *Rolling Stone, Brill's Content, Mother Jones,* and *Playboy.* He is currently a contributor to *Rolling Stone* and writer-at-large for *Playboy.*

Boal's 2003 article "Jailbait," about an undercover drug agent, was adapted for FOX television's *The Inside.* His piece "Death and Dishonor," the true story of a military veteran murdered by his own platoon mates, became the basis for the film *In the Valley of Elah,* on which Boal worked with director Paul Haggis and shares a screen story credit with Haggis. Tommy Lee Jones received an Academy Award® nomination for his role as Hank in the film, *The New Yorker* praised the film's writing for being "a devastating critique of the Iraq war," and it was deemed "a deeply reflective, highly powerful work" by the *Hollywood Reporter.* Boal's 2008 investigative story for *Rolling Stone,* "Everyone Will Remember Me as Some Sort of Monster" about the life and times of mall shooter Robert Hawkins, will be included in the *Best American Crime Writing* anthology, edited by Otto Penzler.

**KATHRYN BIGELOW** (Director and Producer) has distinguished herself as one of Hollywood's most innovative filmmakers. Her most recent directorial achievement, *The Hurt Locker,* was released in June 2009 to become "the most critically acclaimed American film of the year," according to *The New York Times.*

In 1985, Bigelow directed and co-wrote the stirring cult classic *Near Dark,* produced by Steven-Charles Jaffe. The film was critically lauded as a "poetic horror film." As always, Bigelow's visual style garnered positive reactions from the press, who described it as "dreamy, passionate and terrifying, a hallucinatory vision of the American nightworld that becomes both seductive and devastating." Following the release of the film, the Museum of Modern Art honored Bigelow with a career retrospective.

In 1991, Bigelow directed the action thriller *Point Break*, which starred Keanu Reeves and Patrick Swayze. Executive produced by James Cameron, *Point Break* explored the dangerous extremes of a psychological struggle between two young men. *The Chicago Tribune* commended her astonishing filmmaking sensibilities and described her as "a uniquely talented, uniquely powerful filmmaker…Bigelow has tapped into something primal and strong. She is a sensualist in the most sensual of mediums."

When *Strange Days* was released in 1995, Roger Ebert called it a "technical tour de force." In the film, Bigelow explored the unsettling prospects of computer-generated virtual reality and the impending new millennium. *Strange Days* received rave reviews and was highly praised for its energy and unique, intense visuals. Janet Maslin, in *The New York Times*, stated that "the furiously talented" Bigelow was "operating at full throttle… using material ablaze with eerie promise… she turns *Strange Days* into a troubling but undeniably breathless joyride." Starring Ralph Fiennes, Angela Bassett, and Juliette Lewis, *Strange Days* was co-written by James Cameron.

Bigelow also directed *The Weight of Water*, starring Sean Penn, Sarah Polley, Catherine McCormack, and Elizabeth Hurley. Based on the bestselling Anita Shreve novel, The *Weight of Water* made its world premiere in a gala screening at the 25th annual Toronto International Film Festival in 2000 and drew praise from critics and filmmakers alike. *Variety* described the film as being "Bigelow's richest, most ambitious and personal work to date; imbued with suspense, benefiting from Bigelow's penchant for creating a visual sense of menace and an atmosphere of fear."

On the release of *K-19: The Widowmaker*, *The New York Times* declared Bigelow "one of the most gifted…directors working in movies today." Starring Harrison Ford, Liam Neeson, and Peter Saarsgard, it was one of the more critically well-received films of the summer of 2002. The film tells the true story of a heroic Soviet naval crew who risked their lives to prevent a near nuclear disaster aboard their submarine. Critics praised Bigelow as "an expert technician who never steps wrong" (Roger Ebert).